EXCEL FOR SENIORS MADE EASY

Spreadsheet Management Simplified

By James Bernstein

Copyright © 2024 by James Bernstein. All rights reserved.

All rights reserved. This book or any portion thereof
may not be reproduced or used in any manner whatsoever
without the express written permission of the publisher
except for the use of brief quotations in a book review.

Printed in the United States of America

Bernstein, James
Microsoft Excel for Seniors Made Easy
Part of the Computers for Seniors series

For more information on reproducing sections of this book or sales of this book, go to **www.madeeasybookseries.com**

Contents

Introduction 5

Chapter 1 - Microsoft Excel Overview.. 7

   The Excel Interface 7

   The Quick Access Toolbar 9

   The Excel Ribbon 11

   Using the Online Version of Excel 19

Chapter 2 – Working with Excel 22

   Opening and Creating New Workbooks 22

   Using Templates 25

   Adding Data to Your Worksheet 28

   Copying and Moving Data 30

   Inserting Rows and Columns 35

   Adding and Renaming Worksheets 39

   Save Options 41

   Inserting Objects, Tables and Charts 44

   Search Options 62

Chapter 3 – Functions, Formulas and Sorting 66

   Functions 66

   The Formula Bar 72

   Creating Formulas 76

   Sorting Data 82

Chapter 4 – Formatting Your Workbook 87
Adding Cell Borders 87
Adding Colors to Cells 91
Changing Font Attributes 93
Adjusting Cell Width and Height 96
Text Alignment 97
Using Styles and Conditional Formatting 103
Formatting Cells for Numbers 110
Hiding Rows, Columns and Tabs 114
Using the Freeze Panes feature 118
Merging Cells 121

Chapter 5 – Page Layout and Printing 123
Page Setup 123
Page Breaks 125
Printing Worksheets and Workbooks 127
Creating PDF Files 133

What's Next? 140

About the Author 143

Introduction

Spreadsheet software has been around for almost as long as computers themselves. Microsoft came out with their Windows operating system in 1985 and in 1987, Microsoft Excel for Windows was released, and it has been the go to spreadsheet software ever since.

Since Windows and Excel were both created by Microsoft, it makes sense that they would want to push Windows users to use Excel as their spreadsheet software. You might have heard of other word spreadsheet software such as Google Sheets, LibreOffice Calc, and Apple Numbers. Even though these are powerful full featured spreadsheet programs, they are nowhere near as popular as Microsoft Excel.

If you have Excel installed on your computer, you most likely have other Microsoft programs such as Word and PowerPoint installed as well since most of the time, people buy Excel as part of the Microsoft Office suite of apps even though it is possible to buy Excel as a standalone product.

Speaking of Office, you might have heard or read about Office 365. This is Microsoft's subscription-based Office suite that you can use online via your web browser and also as installed programs on your computer. You pay yearly for the subscription but that gets you all the updates for all the Office software as they come out. There is also a free version of Excel and other Office apps you can use online called Office for the Web but it's not as powerful as the Office 365 version yet can be just fine for many users.

In this book, I will be using the desktop version of Excel which most people prefer since it's a bit easier to use and you don't need to worry about storing documents "in the cloud" unless you really want to since it will be an option for you. Once you get the hang of

Chapter 1 - Microsoft Excel Overview

the desktop version of Excel, you should also be able to apply your knowledge to the online version and adapt just fine.

Even though Microsoft Excel is a very powerful program, I will be sticking with the basics so you can learn how to use the major features of Excel and not get overwhelmed by all the advanced tasks you can perform. I will discuss some of the more advanced features just because I think they are important to at least be aware of. Then once you become proficient with the basics, you can then branch out and learn some of the other features if you choose to do so. So on that note, let's start adding some data!

Chapter 1 - Microsoft Excel Overview

If you are reading this book, it's probably safe to assume that you are using or need to start using Microsoft Excel to work with some data. Maybe you are using it for a project at home or an assignment at the office, but no matter where you use the software, it works the same!

Just like with most new things, once you get comfortable using Excel, things will start falling into place and you will start to wonder how you were ever intimated by the software to begin with.

The Excel Interface
The first time you open Excel, it might be a bit overwhelming with all the tabs, buttons and icons. One important thing to keep in mind is that you don't need to know what all these items do since most people never use every feature of Excel. You should only be focusing on the tools and functions you need to use and once you get those down you can worry about the rest.

There are many components that make up the Excel program but for now, I will just be going over the main areas of the interface so you know what you will be working with for the most part. Figure 1.1 shows a blank Excel worksheet with nothing entered in the cells yet. By the way, the boxes where you add your data area are called cells.

Chapter 1 - Microsoft Excel Overview

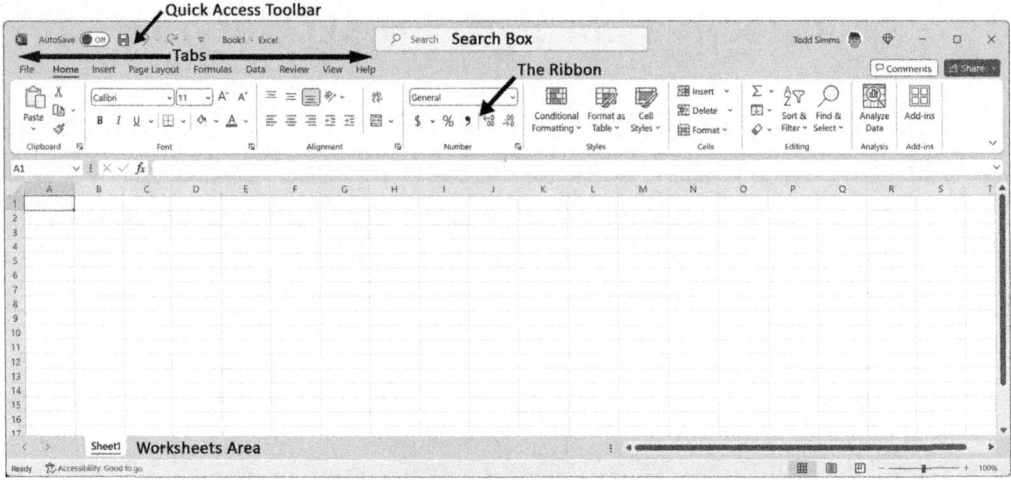

Figure 1.1

You will have rows on the left side and columns on the top. The rows start with the number 1 and the columns start with the letter A. As you go down or to the right, these numbers and letters will increase as you go along. When you get to the letter Z for the columns, the next one will start with AA, AB, AC and so on.

At the upper left of the spreadsheet, you will have the Quick Access Toolbar which will be discussed in the next section. Then below that you have the Excel Ribbon which spans the entire width of the Excel window. This is where you will find most of the tools you will be using to manipulate your data. I will be discussing this after the section on the Quick Access Toolbar.

The Formula Bar is where you can view and type formulas. I will be going over basic formulas in Chapter 3. At the bottom of the window, you will see your worksheets. By default, Excel will have one worksheet called *Sheet1*. You can add more as needed and also rename them. All your worksheets make up the Excel workbook.

To the right of the Quick Access Toolbar, you will find the name of your spreadsheet. The default name is *Book1* until you save it the

Chapter 1 - Microsoft Excel Overview

first time and then you can change the name. If you open another blank workbook, it will be named Book2 and so on.

The Quick Access Toolbar
At the upper left of the Excel window, you will find what is known as the Quick Access Toolbar. This is used to keep shortcuts to the most commonly used commands and tools. That way, you do not need to go find them each time within the Ribbon. By default, the Quick Access Toolbar will have the AutoSave feature, save, undo and redo shortcuts on it. If you were to click on the down arrow to the right of the toolbar, you would see that these options are checked, and you can also select additional commonly used commands from the list to add them to your Quick Access Toolbar (Figure 1.2).

Chapter 1 - Microsoft Excel Overview

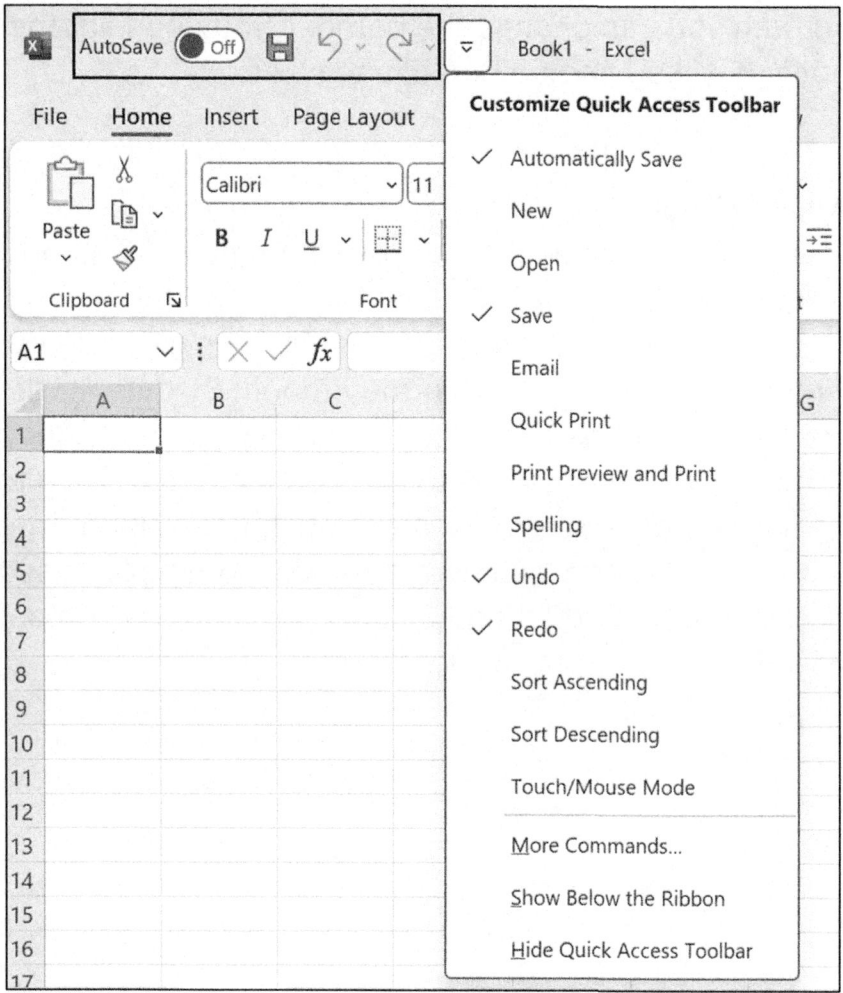
Figure 1.2

For example, if I check the *Open* option, it will then be added to my Quick Access Toolbar as seen in Figure 1.3.

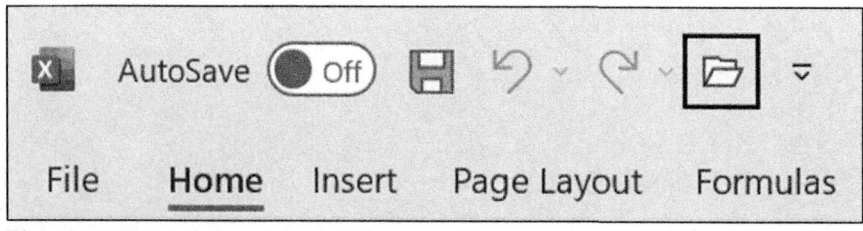
Figure 1.3

Chapter 1 - Microsoft Excel Overview

If you do not like the Quick Access Toolbar at the top of the Excel window, you can have it placed underneath the ribbon by choosing that option from the dropdown menu.

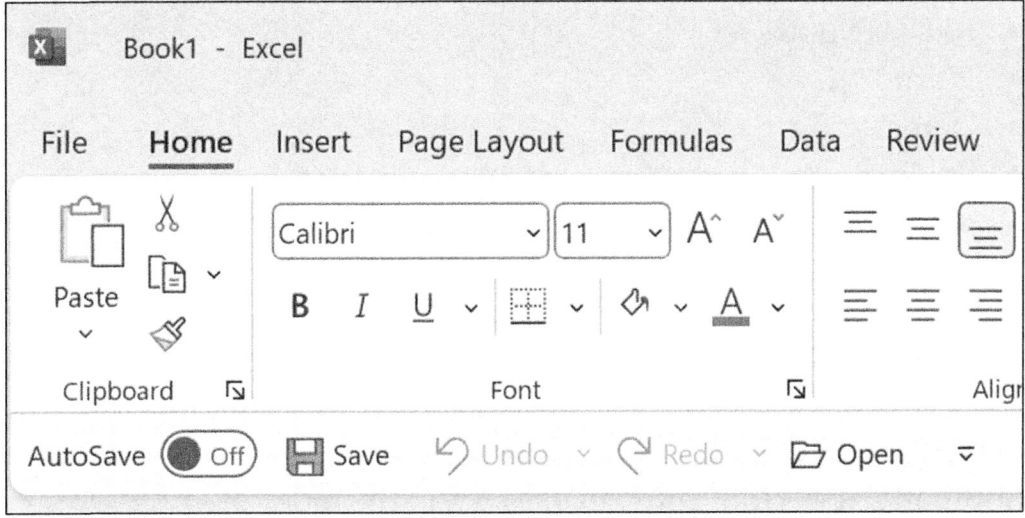

Figure 1.4

You can also hide the Quick Access Toolbar by unchecking the box that says *Show Quick Access Toolbar*.

The Excel Ribbon

Starting with Office 2007, Microsoft added the Ribbon feature to its Office software as a new and improved way to use all the tools and functions built into the various Office programs.

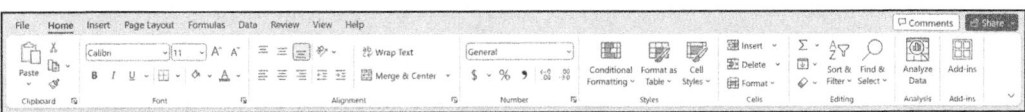

Figure 1.5

The Ribbon is broken up into various categories that can be accessed by clicking on the tab name above the Ribbon itself. In previous versions of Office, these tabs looked more like actual tabs, but people still refer to them as tabs.

Chapter 1 - Microsoft Excel Overview

The default tabs for Excel include the following.
- File
- Home
- Insert
- Page Layout
- Formulas
- Data
- Review
- View
- Help

Occasionally, you will see additional tabs when you do certain things in Excel. For example, if you were to insert a picture into your spreadsheet, you would then see a *Picture Format* tab with some additional tools that you can use to edit the picture.

When you click on a particular tab, the items on the Ribbon will change to reflect the tools included in that category. Figure 1.6 shows what happens when I click on the Home tab and Figure 1.7 shows what happens when I click on the Insert tab.

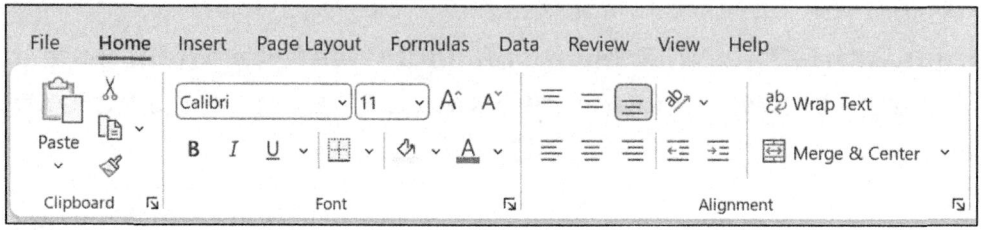
Figure 1.6

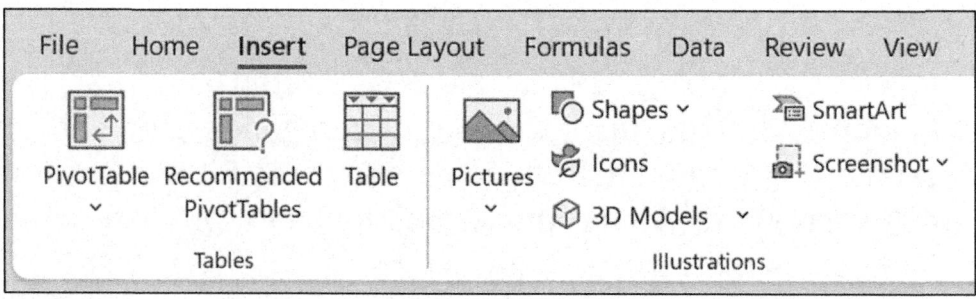
Figure 1.7

Chapter 1 - Microsoft Excel Overview

The sections within the Ribbon are referred to as *Groups*. In Figure 1.7, you can see the Tables and Illustrations groups.

Some groups will have additional options that can be accessed by clicking on the arrow icon at the lower right corner of the group as seen in Figures 1.8 and 1.9.

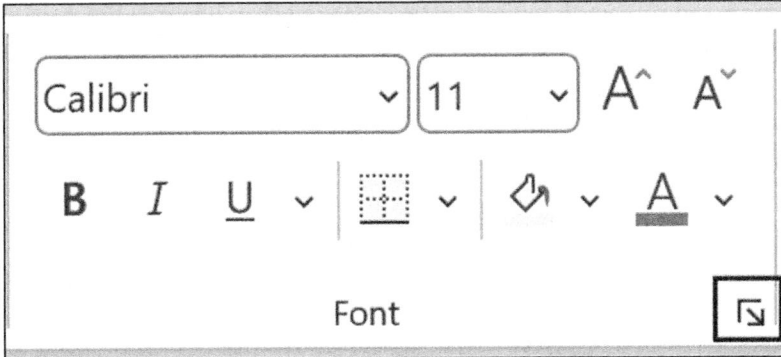

Figure 1.8

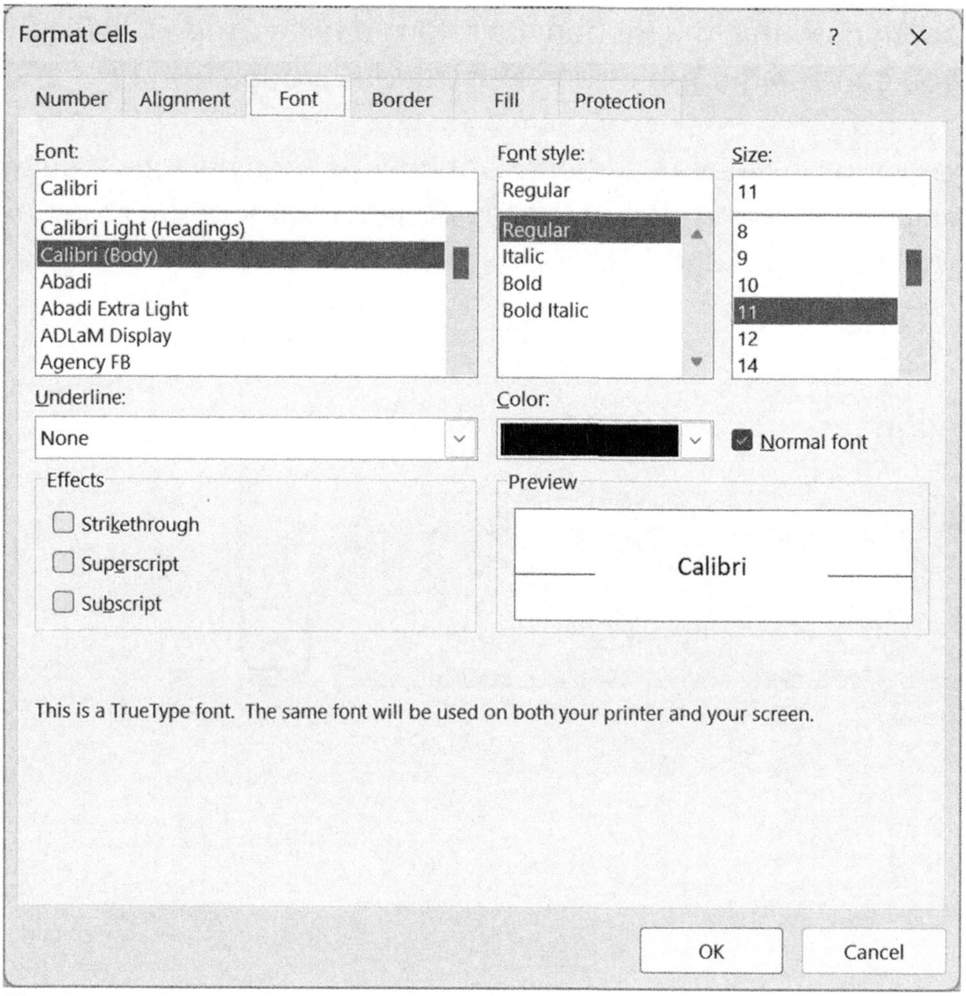

Chapter 1 - Microsoft Excel Overview

Figure 1.9

I will now go over each of the tabs in the Ribbon and give a brief overview of what kinds of tools you can find in each one.

File
The File tab is a bit different from the other tabs in Excel because it does not contain any tools like you will find in other tabs on the Ribbon. Rather you will come here to do things such as save your workbook or save it with a different name or in a different folder (save as).

Chapter 1 - Microsoft Excel Overview

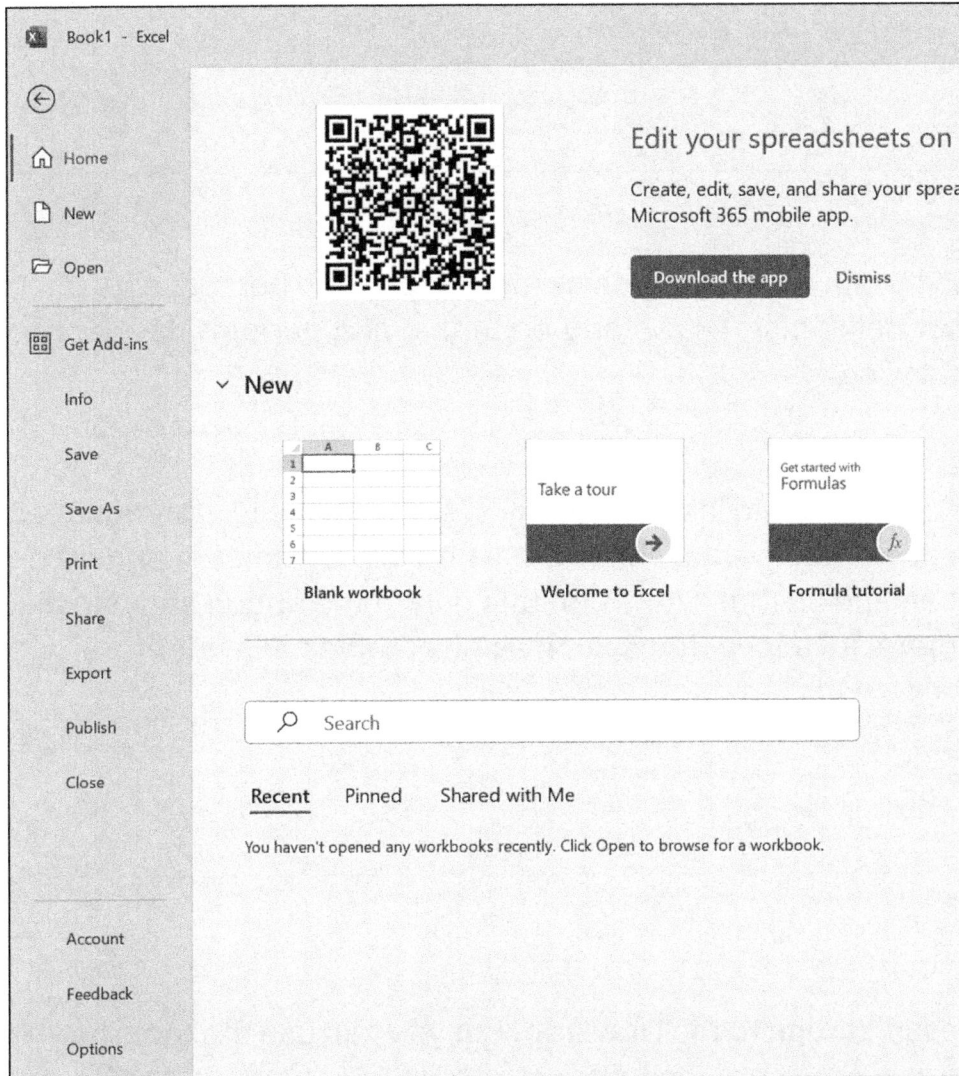

Figure 1.10

You will also come to the File section to print, share, or export your workbook if you need to. If you need to find information about your Microsoft 365 subscription or Excel version, you can find that here as well.

Home
The Home tab is where you will most likely find yourself until you get to be more of an advanced Excel user. It is similar to the Home tab in Microsoft Word and has many of the same tools.

Chapter 1 - Microsoft Excel Overview

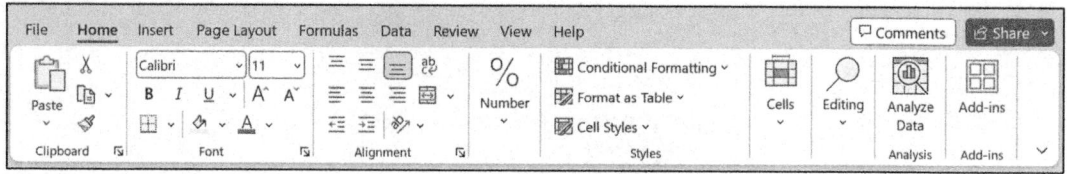

Figure 1.11

Here you can do things such as format text, add borders and colors to your cells, insert rows and columns, and perform data sorting and filtering.

Insert
Excel allows you to insert a variety of things into your spreadsheets such as photos, tables, charts, text boxes, comments and so on. You can find all these items on this part of the ribbon and can also add more advanced items such as pivot tables and filters.

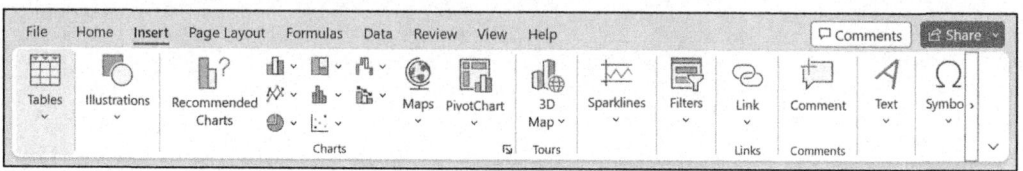

Figure 1.12

Draw
There isn't much to the Draw tab, but you can use the tools here to markup your spreadsheet with "virtual" pens, pencils and highlighters. The *Convert* group contains tools you can use to convert drawings like a box into an actual shape or a handwritten formula into math that can be used within your spreadsheet.

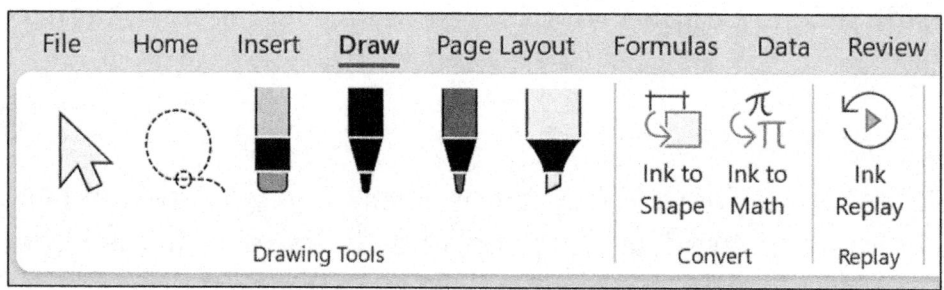

Figure 1.13

16

Chapter 1 - Microsoft Excel Overview

Page Layout

The tools in the Page Layout tab are essential to know if you plan on printing or exporting your spreadsheet to something like a PDF. Here you can change things such as page margins, size and orientation. You can also set scaling settings to make your data fit on a certain number of pages. If you want the gridlines to appear on the screen or when you print, you can change these settings from here as well. Gridlines are different from cell borders.

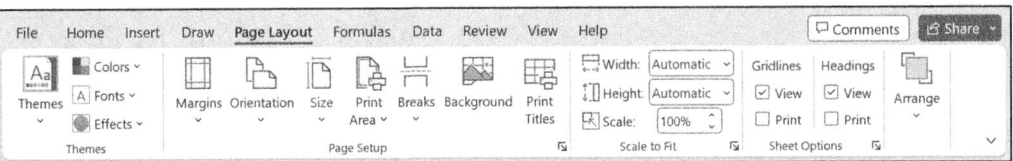

Figure 1.14

Formulas

I will be discussing formulas in Chapter 3, but for now, you should know that you can come to the Formulas tab to insert custom formulas, view the formula library, audit your formulas and perform other advanced data calculations. By the way, there is a good chance that you will never need to use a formula!

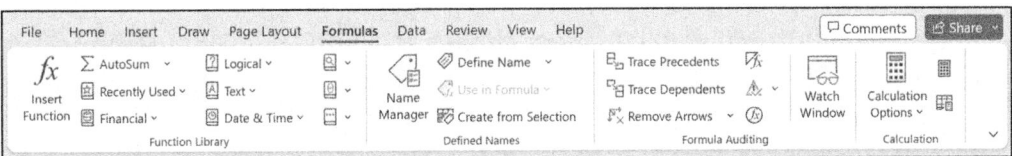

Figure 1.15

Data

Excel is all about manipulating data and the Data tab is where you will find a variety of tools to work with your data to make it work for you. Here you can do things such as run queries and sort and filter your data.

Chapter 1 - Microsoft Excel Overview

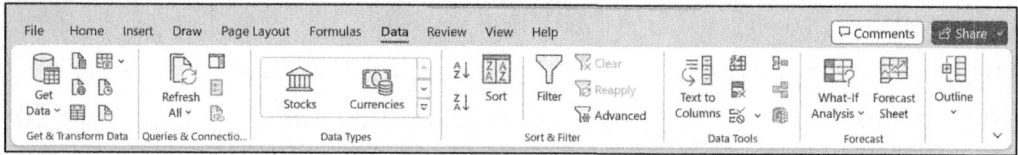

Figure 1.16

Review

Just like with Microsoft Word, Excel has tools you can use to make sure your workbook and its data are correct and accessible to anyone who might be using your spreadsheet. There is a built-in spell checker and accessibility checker you can use to help you accomplish this. If you have a reason to lock or password protect your workbook, you can do so here as well.

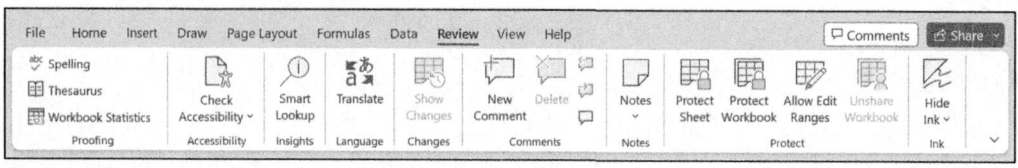

Figure 1.17

View

The View tab contains many tools you can use to change how your worksheet appears on the screen. The default view is *Normal,* but you can also change it to *Page Break Preview* to help make sure your data is on the page you want it to be before printing it out. You can also change the zoom level from here and this can also be done from the zoom slider at the lower right corner of the Excel interface.

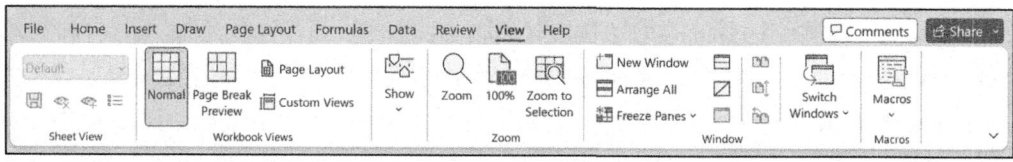

Figure 1.18

Chapter 1 - Microsoft Excel Overview

Using the Online Version of Excel

Most people who use Excel prefer the desktop version that you install and run from your computer. There is a version for Windows and also for Mac. But if you are on another device that doesn't have Excel installed, there is no need to worry because you can also run it from a web browser on almost any device with an internet connection.

To access the online version of Excel, and other Office apps like Word and Outlook, you just need to go to the **office.com** website and log in with your Microsoft account. If you are a Windows user, you already have a Microsoft account, so you just need to remember the email address and password associated with it!

After you log in, you will see the main Microsoft 365 page and if you see a button that says Buy Microsoft 365, that means you are using the free version, and your Microsoft account is not tied to a Microsoft 365 paid subscription (Figure 1.19).

Chapter 1 - Microsoft Excel Overview

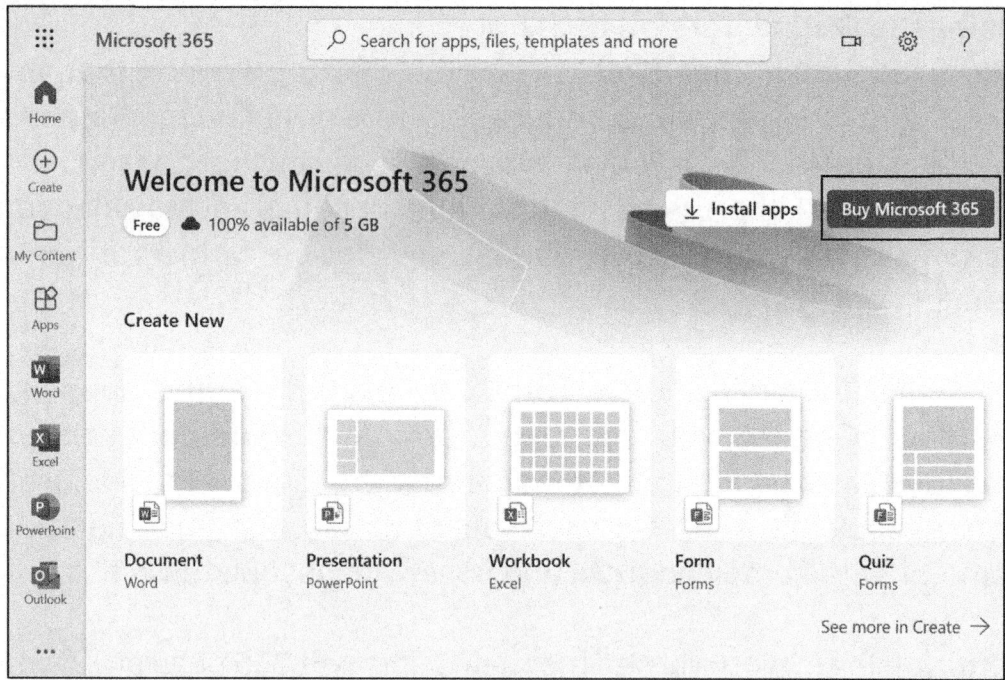

Figure 1.19

When you buy Office, you can use the full featured online version as well as the desktop versions of the apps.

The free online version of Excel and other Office apps do not have all the features as the pay for version but for most "regular" Excel users, it has everything you need to get the job done.

Figure 1.20 shows the online version of Excel running in a web browser. Overall, it looks very similar to the desktop version, but you will notice that the Ribbon is more compact and does not have as many tools on it.

Chapter 1 - Microsoft Excel Overview

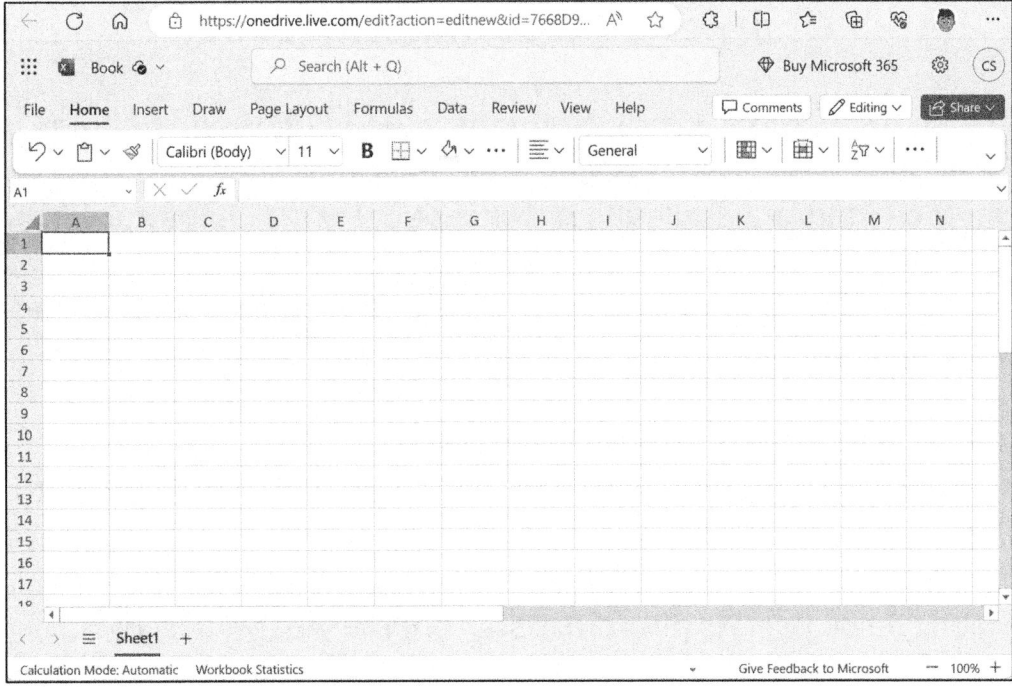

Figure 1.20

If you click on the down arrow at the very right of the Ribbon, you will have the option to use *Classic Ribbon* which shows you more of the available tools for each tab.

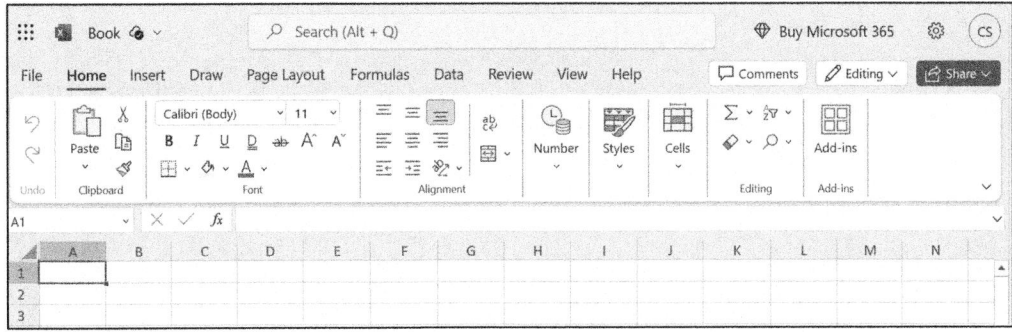

Figure 1.21

Chapter 2 – Working with Excel

Now that you know where to find the various tools and features in Excel, it's time to start adding some data to our workbook so we can then start manipulating it as needed. In this chapter, I will be covering how to create a spreadsheet as well as how to perform the more common tasks that you will be doing when you are working on your own workbooks.

Opening and Creating New Workbooks
When you first open Excel, you will most likely be taken to the *Home* page which will show you any recent workbooks that you have previously worked on. There is also a section labeled *Pinned* which can be used to pin spreadsheet names to this list so you can open them quickly without having to search for them. You can think of this as being similar to a bookmark in your web browser. At the top of this screen, you will also have the option to open a new blank workbook or open a template which will be discussed in the next section.

Chapter 2 – Working with Excel

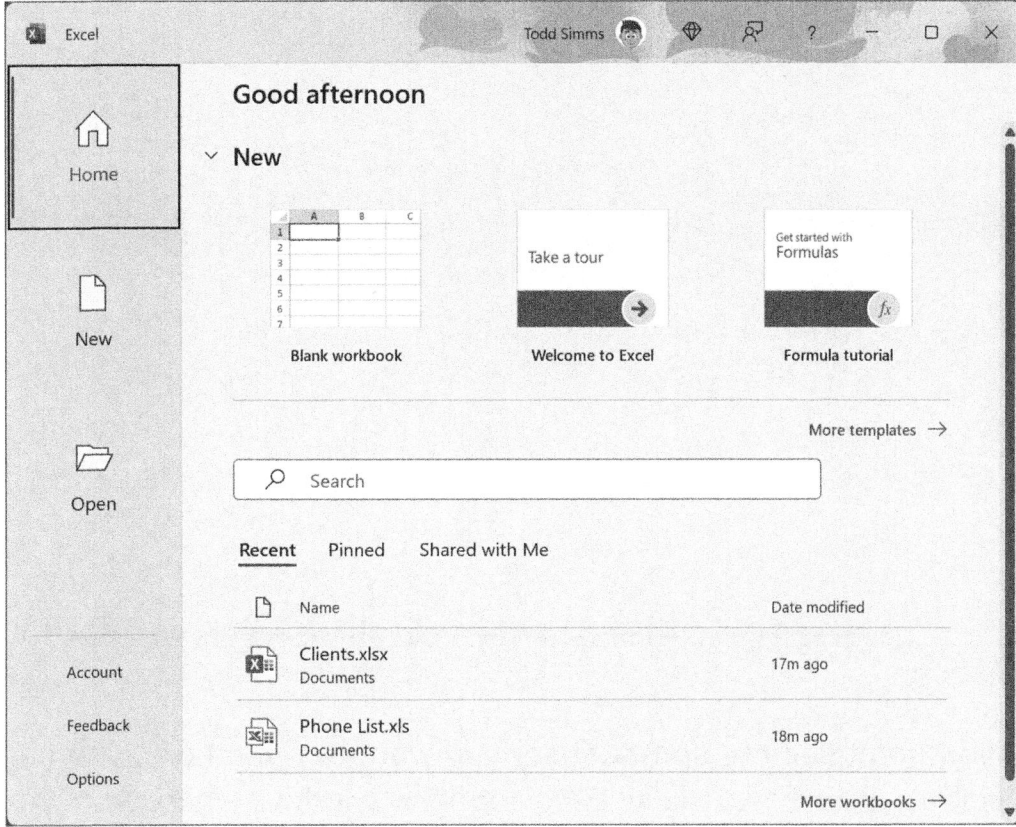

Figure 2.1

Clicking on *Open* will show you your recent and pinned files as well (Figure 2.2). If you click on *Folders*, you will be shown any folders that you recently opened spreadsheets from in case you want to access one from there.

Chapter 2 – Working with Excel

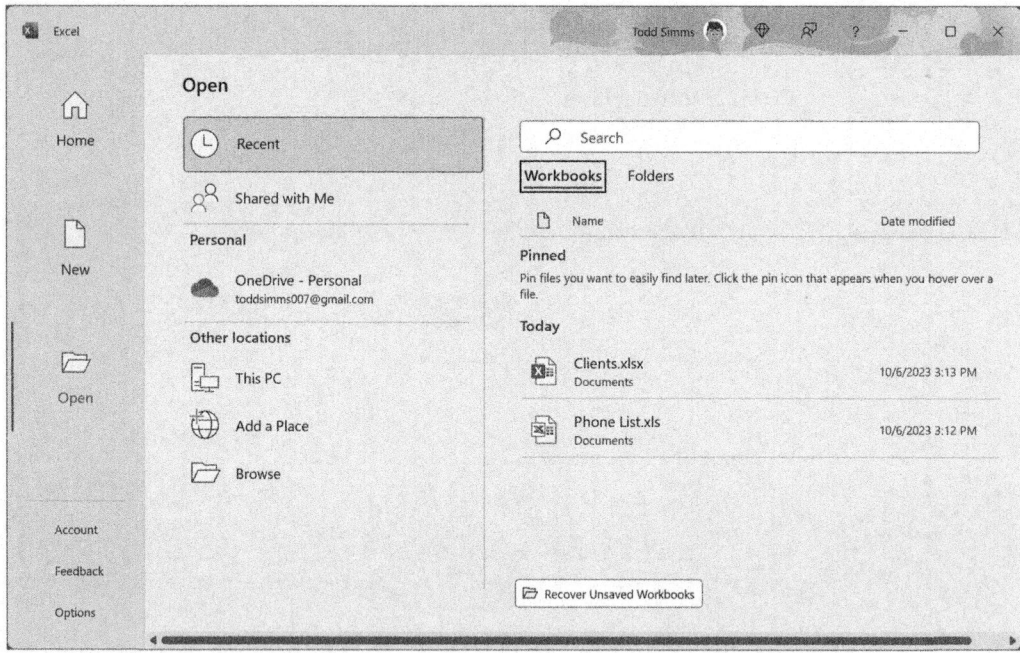

Figure 2.2

If you don't see the spreadsheet you want to open here, you can click on *Browse* to have Excel open a window where you can manually find your workbook on your computer.

Clicking on *New* will give you an option to open a new blank workbook or template just like you saw in the Home section.

Chapter 2 – Working with Excel

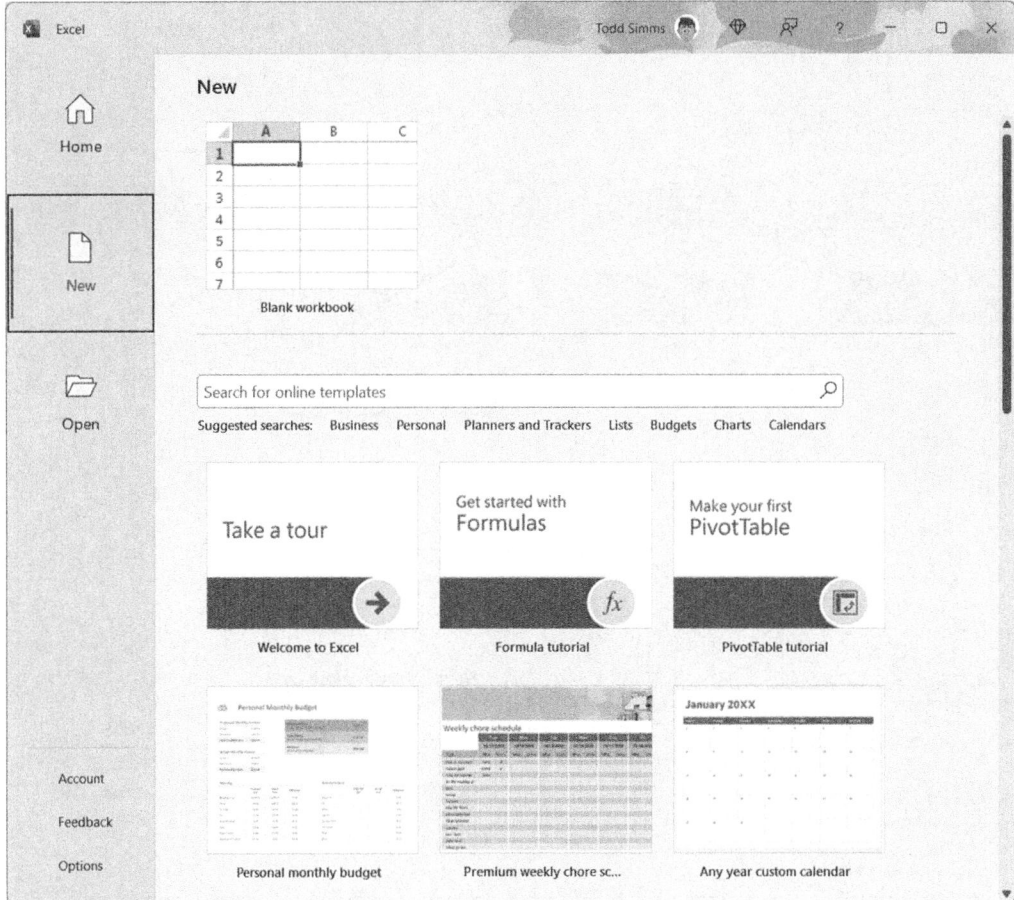

Figure 2.3

Using Templates

Before I get into starting from a blank workbook in Excel, I want to take a moment to go over templates and how to use them. Templates are preconfigured workbooks that have things such as data and formatting already applied to them. Once you open a template, all you need to do is add or remove data as needed so the spreadsheet works the way you need it to.

From the *Home* section, you can click on *More Templates* and view the suggested templates, view the included categories, or do a search for templates.

Chapter 2 – Working with Excel

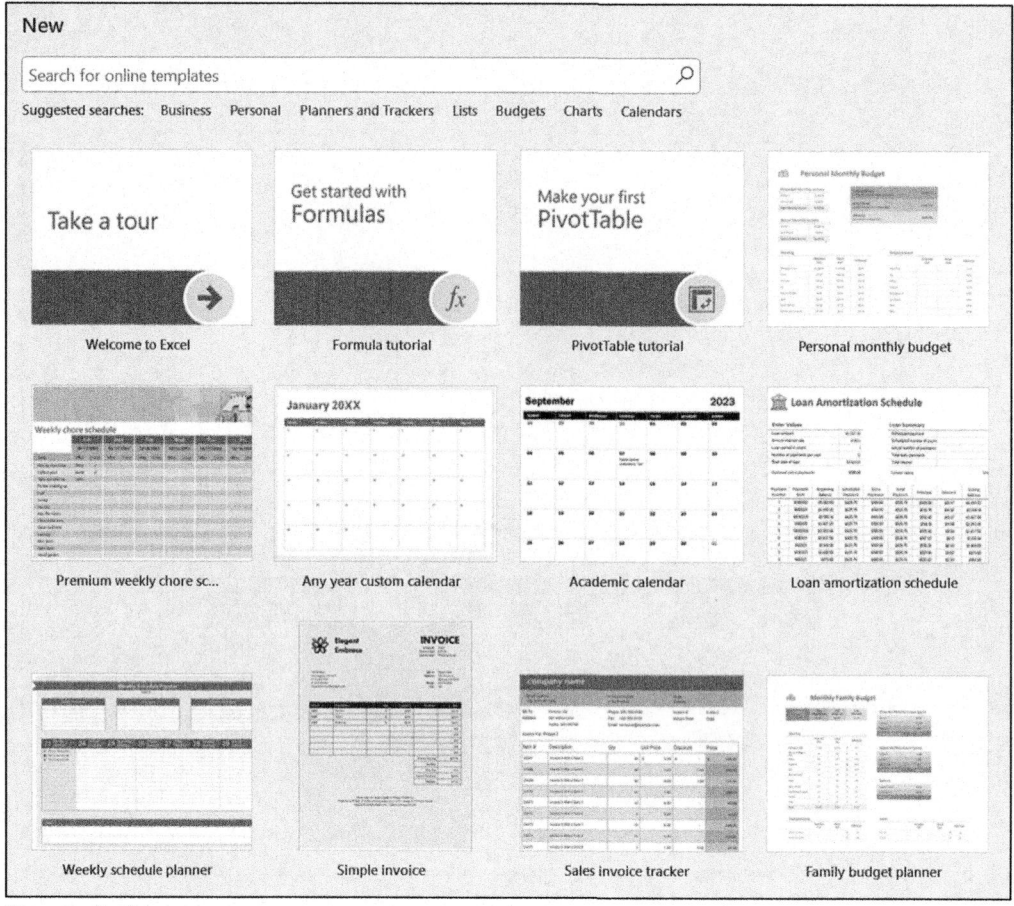

Figure 2.4

I will simply click on the *Personal monthly budget* template and then Excel will ask if I want to download and create the spreadsheet within Excel.

Chapter 2 – Working with Excel

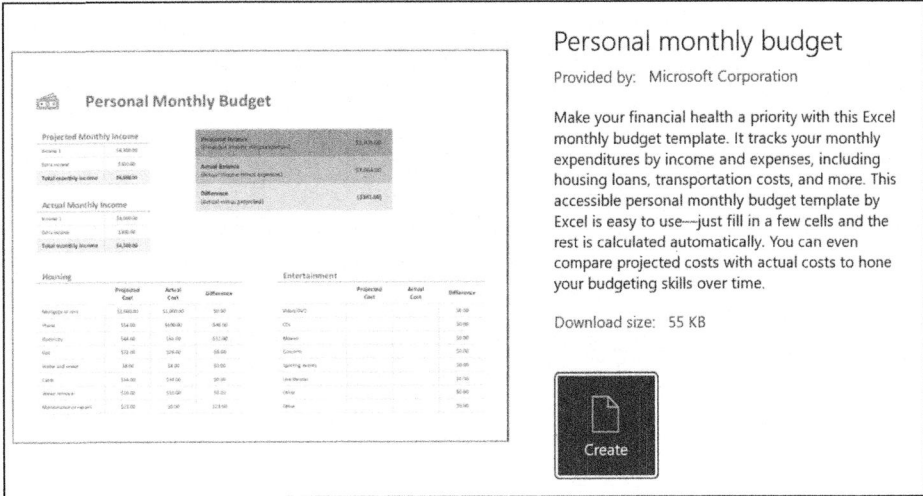

Figure 2.5

Once the template is open in Excel, you can then work on it just like any other spreadsheet and save it with a different name or keep the name that Excel gives to it which should match the template name itself.

Chapter 2 – Working with Excel

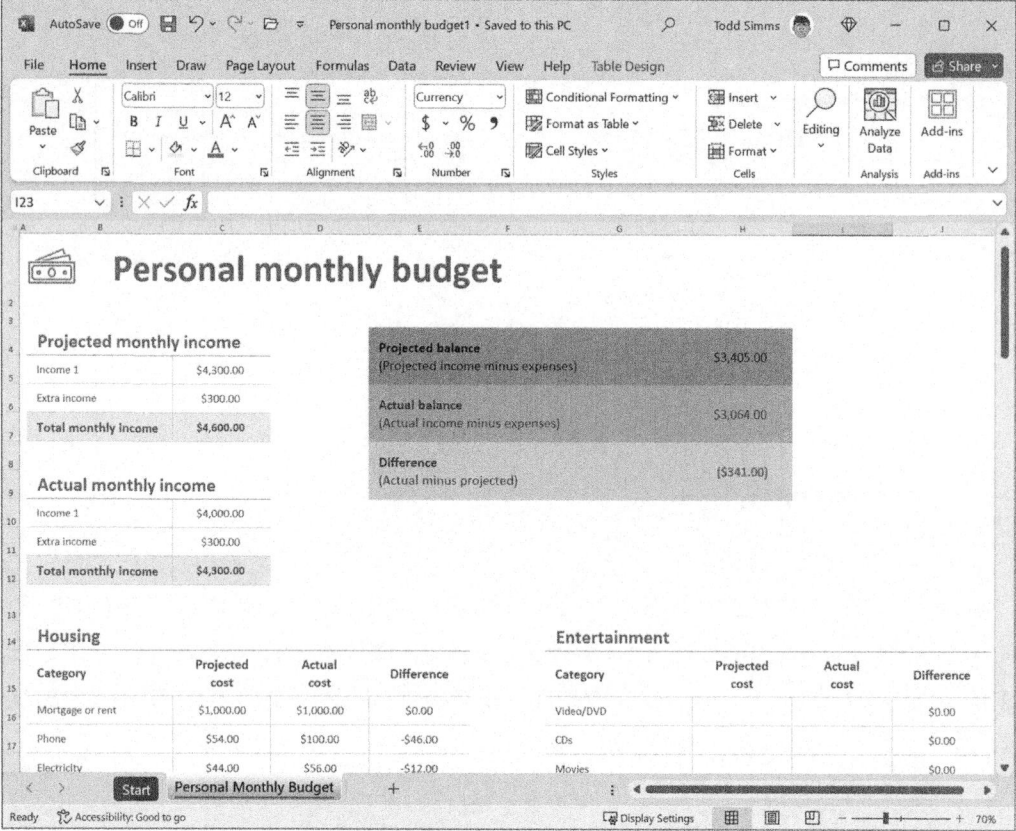

Figure 2.6

Adding Data to Your Worksheet

Now it's time to enter our data into our workbook so we can manipulate it as needed to make it easier to analyze and work with. Data can be in the form of text, numbers, currency, fractions, dates, time and so on. The type of data you enter into your worksheet will determine what you can do with it.

Figure 2.7 shows a blank worksheet with cell A1 selected. The top columns of an Excel worksheet are designated with letters and once you get to the letter Z, the columns will then start with AA, AB, AC and so on. Rows are on the left side of the worksheet and start with the number 1 and continue further than you will ever need to go.

Chapter 2 – Working with Excel

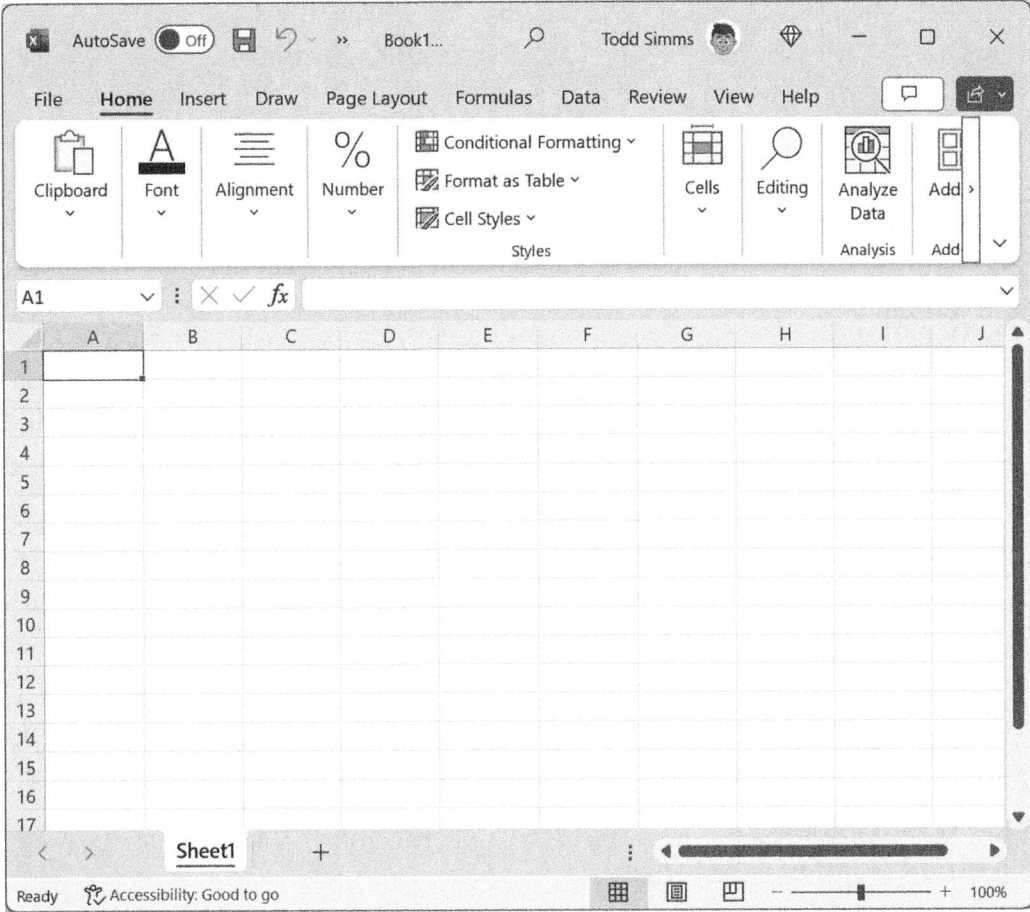

Figure 2.7

To add data to a cell, simply click within that cell and start typing. You can even paste in text or numbers from other sources such as documents or other spreadsheets. As you type, you will see that the cell contents spill into the next cell over (Figure 2.8). This doesn't mean that the data is contained in the other cells but simply just appears that way until you adjust the column to make the data fit.

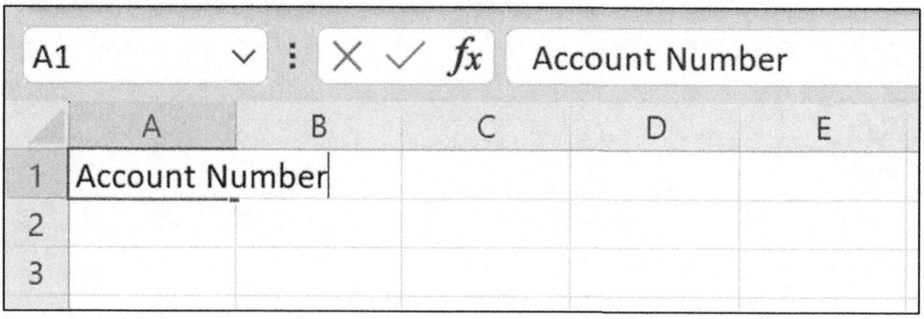

Chapter 2 – Working with Excel

Figure 2.8

At the top of Figure 2.8, you can also see that the same text is in the box at the top of the image that is in the cell itself. This box is called the Formula bar and it's where you can see what formula is contained in a cell. I will be discussing the Formula bar in Chapter 3. When there is no formula in a cell, it will just display the text or numbers from the selected cell.

When you enter data into a cell, you can press the Enter key on your keyboard to be taken to the next cell below or the Tab key to be taken to the next cell to the right. You can also use the arrow keys to move up, down, left or right.

Copying and Moving Data
If you have data from another source that you would like to add to your spreadsheet, you can do things such as import it from another file or simply copy and paste it from one location to another. You can also copy and move data between cells in your worksheet or from one worksheet to another.

Let's say I had a grocery list in a Word document that I wanted to add to my Excel spreadsheet. I could simply highlight and copy the text from Word (on the left of Figure 2.9), click on cell A1 in Excel, and then paste it in. As you can see, the text copied over fine but entries for *Grocery List* and *Paper towels* look like they are spilling over into column B even though they are technically in column A.

Chapter 2 – Working with Excel

Grocery List		A	B
Eggs	1	**Grocery List**	
Milk	2	Eggs	
Bread	3	Milk	
Cheese	4	Bread	
Meat	5	Cheese	
Milk	6	Meat	
Apples	7	Milk	
Lettuce	8	Apples	
Cereal	9	Lettuce	
Paper towels	10	Cereal	
	11	Paper towels	

Figure 2.9

To fix the layout of my text in my spreadsheet, I can simply hold the mouse between the two cells in the grey area between A and B, so it makes a double arrow as seen in Figure 2.10. Then I can click and hold to expand the size of column A so all the text will fit (Figure 2.11).

Chapter 2 – Working with Excel

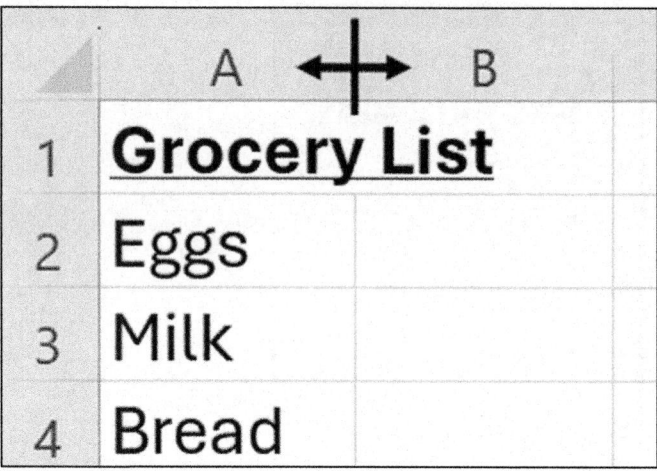

Figure 2.10

	A	B
1	**Grocery List**	
2	Eggs	
3	Milk	
4	Bread	
5	Cheese	
6	Meat	
7	Milk	
8	Apples	
9	Lettuce	
10	Cereal	
11	Paper towels	
12		

Figure 2.11

Chapter 2 – Working with Excel

Another problem you might have is when you are pasting text that might have some formatting applied that you may not want to have applied to your spreadsheet. When this happens, you can then use one of the special paste options. Figure 2.12 shows some text with an unusual font applied to it. This text would not fit well in my spreadsheet and if I were to just do a straightforward copy and paste, I would get the results shown in Figure 2.13.

ACCOUNT NUMBER

Figure 2.12

Figure 2.13

To get around this, I can click in the cell where I would like to place the text and then go to the Home tab and click on the *Paste* button and click on the clipboard icon for plain text (Figure 2.14). The clipboard with the paintbrush on it is for the *match destination formatting* option which will try and make your pasted text match the look of your existing text. I can also click on *Paste special* and then choose the *Text* option (Figure 2.15).

Chapter 2 – Working with Excel

Figure 2.14

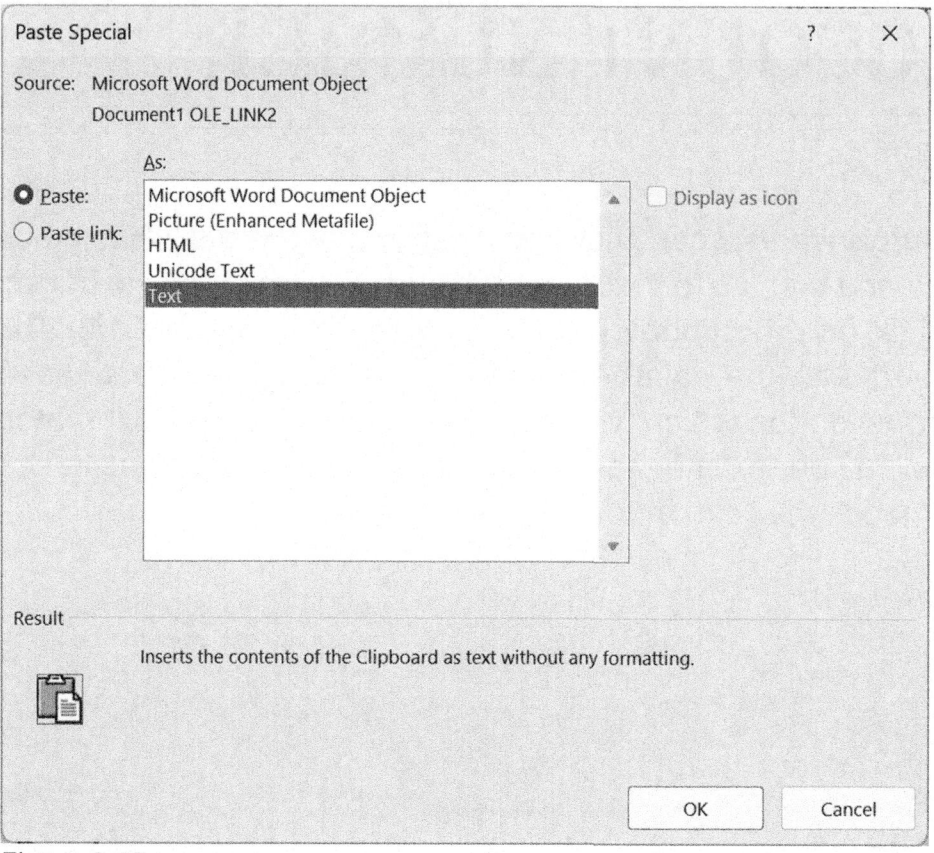
Figure 2.15

Figure 2.16 shows how my text looks when I use the *match destination formatting* option. As you can see, the text in column C1 is using the same font as the other text but Excel did not make it bold like the First Name and Last Name column headers so this is something you will need to watch for so you can manually make any changes that are needed.

	A	B	C
1	**First Name**	**Last Name**	Account Number
2	Vanessa	Watson	
3	Dylan	Bond	
4	Nathan	Morgan	
5	Christian	Clarkson	

Figure 2.16

You can move or copy data between cells in a worksheet or between different worksheets within a workbook just by either cutting and pasting, copying and pasting or dragging and dropping data from one cell or cells to another.

Inserting Rows and Columns
Just because you see certain rows and columns on your worksheet doesn't mean that they are all you can use. Excel will let you add additional rows and columns at any position you need within your spreadsheet.

For the worksheet shown in Figure 2.20, I need a new column between *Account Number* and *Amount* because I want to add some new data between those two sections.

Chapter 2 – Working with Excel

	A	B	C	D	E
1	**First Name**	**Last Name**	**Account Number**	Amount	Send a Bill?
2	Vanessa	Watson	5232148	$121.52	Yes
3	Dylan	Bond	4251575	$83.25	Yes
4	Nathan	Morgan	6562541	$53.87	Yes
5	Christian	Clarkson	4523217	$75.25	Yes
6	Victoria	Dyer	4515482	$101.00	Yes
7	Abigail	Randall	3625145	$112.25	Yes
8	Claire	Ogden	3265147	$86.21	Yes
9	Jan	Clark	9562147	$97.24	Yes
10	Connor	Mathis	3265147	$118.32	Yes
11	Jessica	McGrath	2233517	$198.98	Yes
12	Brian	Randall	9532214	$58.21	Yes
13	Natalie	Baker	9215714	$136.84	Yes
14	Cameron	Welch	3215412	$147.98	Yes
15	Anthony	Lewis	8762514	$26.25	Yes
16	Luke	Simpson	5621514	$89.27	Yes
17	Amy	Avery	7563214	$139.75	Yes
18	Neil	Graham	2124214	$205.63	Yes

Figure 2.17

To do so, I can select the column to the right of where I want to add my new column. Then I can right click on the column letter and choose *Insert* from the menu that appears.

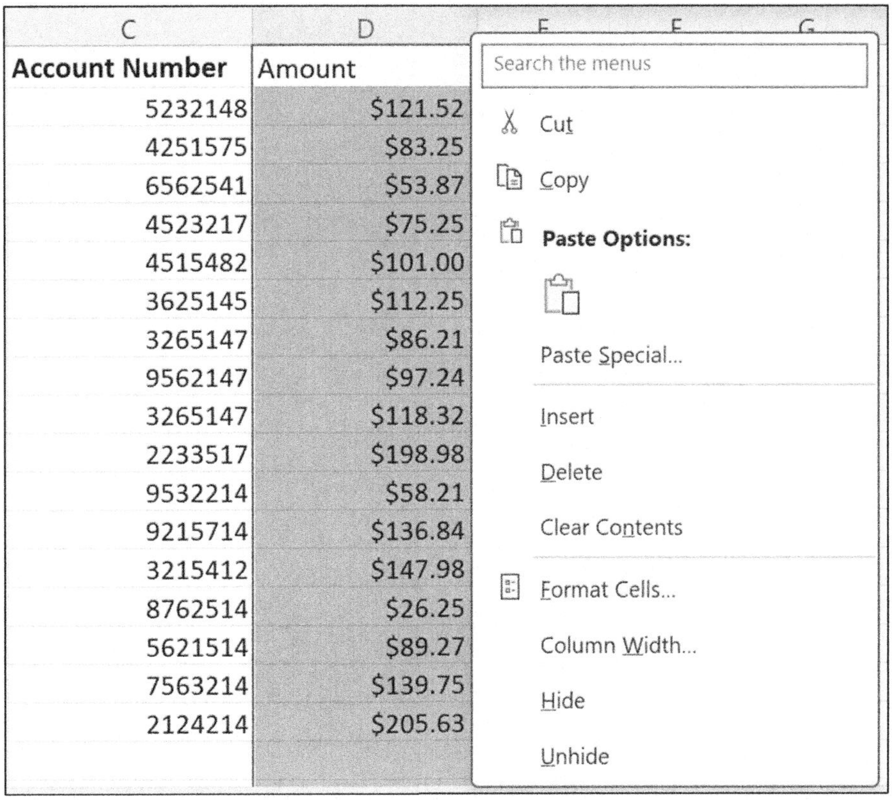

Chapter 2 – Working with Excel

C	D	E	F	G
Account Number	Amount			
5232148	$121.52			
4251575	$83.25			
6562541	$53.87			
4523217	$75.25			
4515482	$101.00			
3625145	$112.25			
3265147	$86.21			
9562147	$97.24			
3265147	$118.32			
2233517	$198.98			
9532214	$58.21			
9215714	$136.84			
3215412	$147.98			
8762514	$26.25			
5621514	$89.27			
7563214	$139.75			
2124214	$205.63			

Context menu options: Search the menus, Cut, Copy, Paste Options:, Paste Special..., Insert, Delete, Clear Contents, Format Cells..., Column Width..., Hide, Unhide

Figure 2.18

I can also highlight the column and go to the *Cells* group within the *Home* tab and choose *Insert* and then *Insert Sheet Columns* (Figure 2.19).

Chapter 2 – Working with Excel

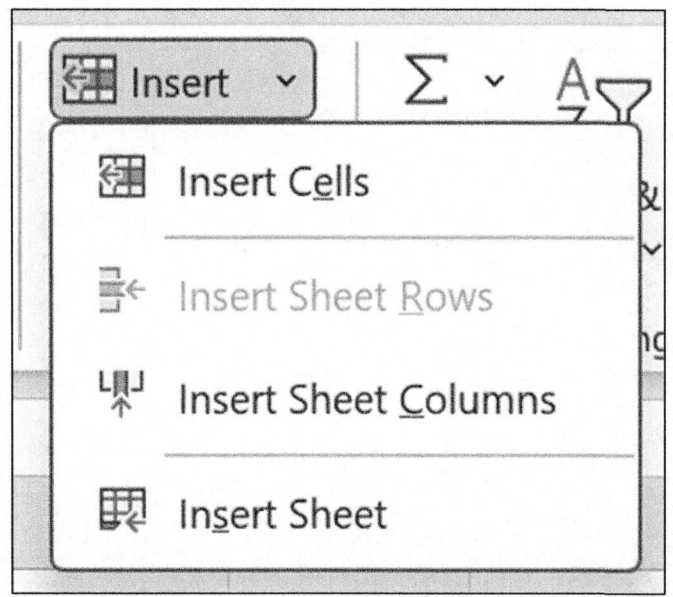

Figure 2.19

Now you can see that I have a new empty column within my worksheet (column D). I can then add new data or copy or move over data from a different column on this worksheet or on another worksheet or even a completely different Excel file altogether.

	A	B	C	D	E	F
1	First Name	Last Name	Account Number		Amount	Send a Bill?
2	Vanessa	Watson	5232148		$121.52	Yes
3	Dylan	Bond	4251575		$83.25	Yes
4	Nathan	Morgan	6562541		$53.87	Yes
5	Christian	Clarkson	4523217		$75.25	Yes
6	Victoria	Dyer	4515482		$101.00	Yes
7	Abigail	Randall	3625145		$112.25	Yes
8	Claire	Ogden	3265147		$86.21	Yes
9	Jan	Clark	9562147		$97.24	Yes
10	Connor	Mathis	3265147		$118.32	Yes
11	Jessica	McGrath	2233517		$198.98	Yes
12	Brian	Randall	9532214		$58.21	Yes
13	Natalie	Baker	9215714		$136.84	Yes
14	Cameron	Welch	3215412		$147.98	Yes
15	Anthony	Lewis	8762514		$26.25	Yes
16	Luke	Simpson	5621514		$89.27	Yes
17	Amy	Avery	7563214		$139.75	Yes
18	Neil	Graham	2124214		$205.63	Yes

Figure 2.20

Chapter 2 – Working with Excel

To add a new row to your worksheet, you can use the same process but will need to select the row below where you want the new row to go.

Adding and Renaming Worksheets

When you create a new blank workbook, Excel will include one worksheet with the default name of *Sheet1*. If you only need one worksheet then this should be fine but if you want to separate your data into multiple worksheets, you can easily add additional sheets to your workbook. To do so, click on the **+** button next to Sheet1 and Excel will add a new worksheet called Sheet2 (Figure 2.22). You can add additional sheets as needed whenever you like.

17	Amy	Avery
18	Neil	Graham
19		

Sheet1

Figure 2.21

You can then toggle between each worksheet by clicking on its name on the worksheet tab.

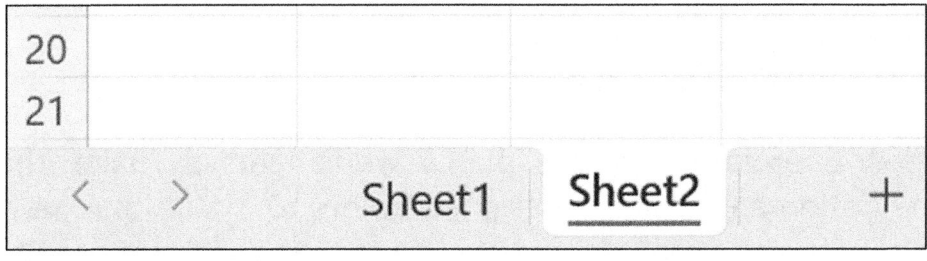

20
21

Sheet1 Sheet2

Figure 2.22

Chapter 2 – Working with Excel

If you would like to organize things further, you can rename your worksheets and do things such as change their color etc. To do so, right click on the worksheet name and you will have several options as seen in Figure 2.23.

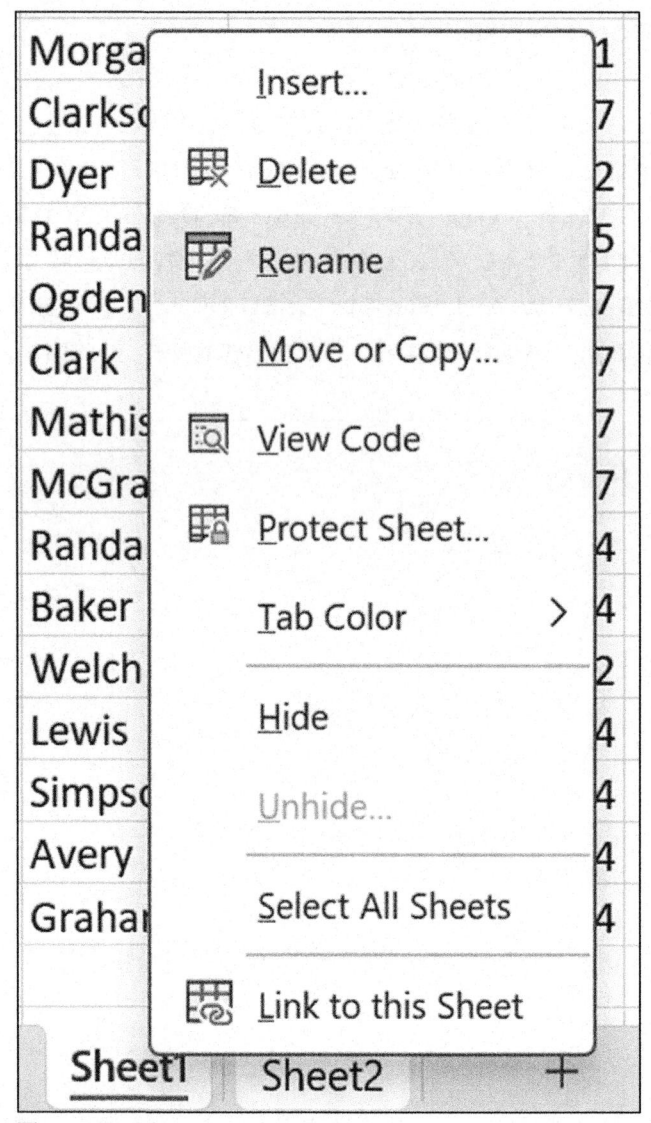

Figure 2.23

I will now change the names of my worksheets by using the *Rename* option and also change their colors to match their new names by using the *Tab Color* option. Figure 2.24 shows the results of these changes.

Chapter 2 – Working with Excel

Figure 2.24

To rearrange your worksheets, you can simply drag and drop them in whichever order you like as needed.

Save Options
Before getting too much further in the workbook creation process, I want to go over some of the save options you have for Excel. Just like with any other program you are using to create files, you will need to save on a regular basis to ensure the safety of your data in case the program or your computer crashes. On a side note, when using the online version of Excel or other Office apps, your progress is saved in real time so there is no need to click on a save button.

If you have not saved your spreadsheet yet, you can go to the *File* tab and then click on *Save* (or press Ctrl-s on your keyboard). If you have saved your spreadsheet and want to change the name or the save location, you can click on *Save As*, but either choice will take you to the Save As option page.

Once you are here, you can type in a name for your spreadsheet in the box at the upper right where it says *Enter file name here*. Below that, you may or may not see some recently used folders that you can choose if you want to save your file in one of these. You can also click the *New Folder* button to create a new folder in a location of your choosing.

The *OneDrive* option at the top is used to save your files in the cloud using the Microsoft OneDrive cloud storage feature. If you are not careful, Excel and other Office programs will try and save

Chapter 2 – Working with Excel

your files there because Microsoft wants you to use OneDrive for some reason.

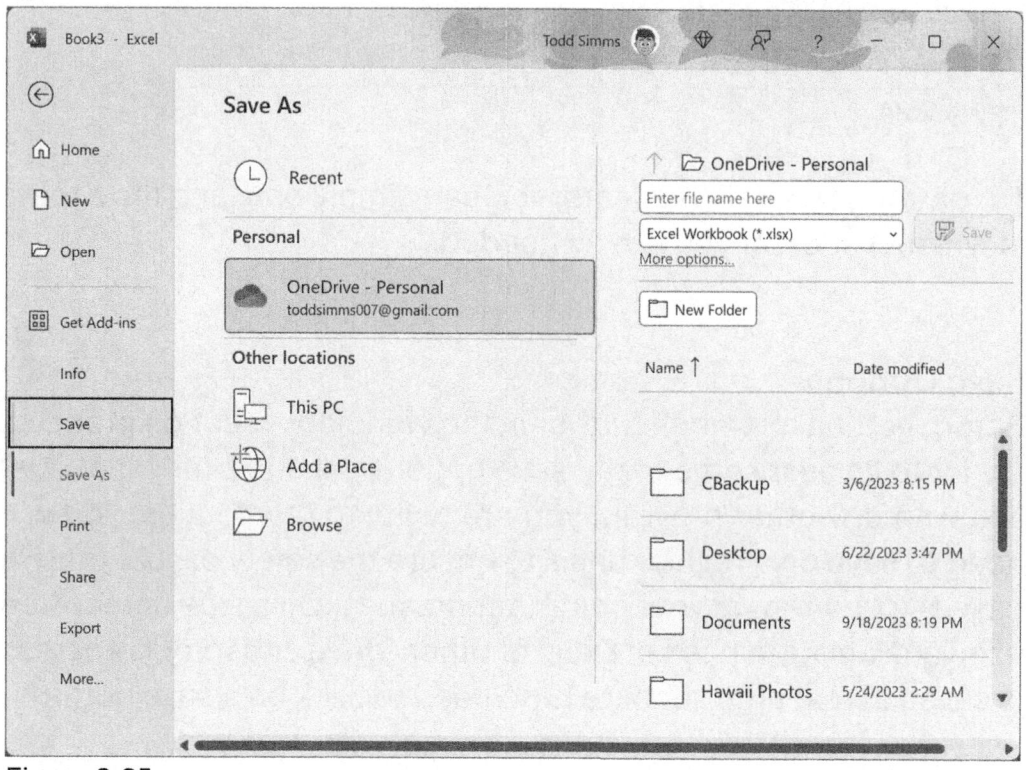

Figure 2.25

If you already have a folder that you would like to save your file in, you can click on *More options* or *Browse* to be given the option to navigate to the folder where you wish to save the file (Figure 2.26). Then you can change the name of the file as needed and click the *Save* button when you are finished.

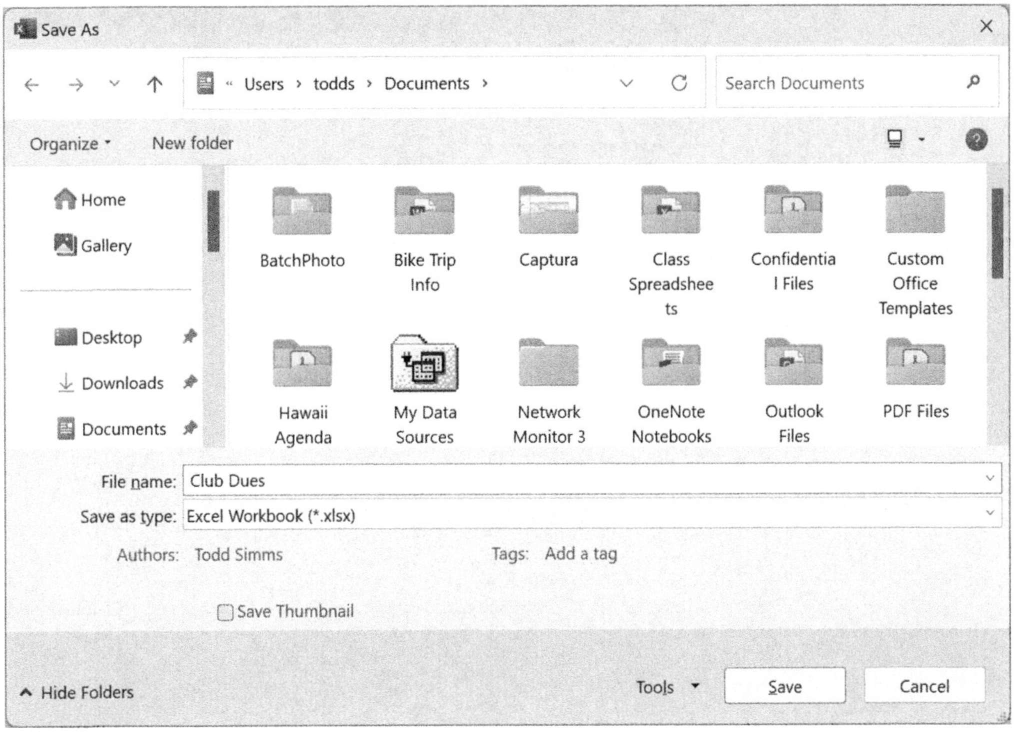

Figure 2.26

Now you will see the name of your file at the top of the Excel window.

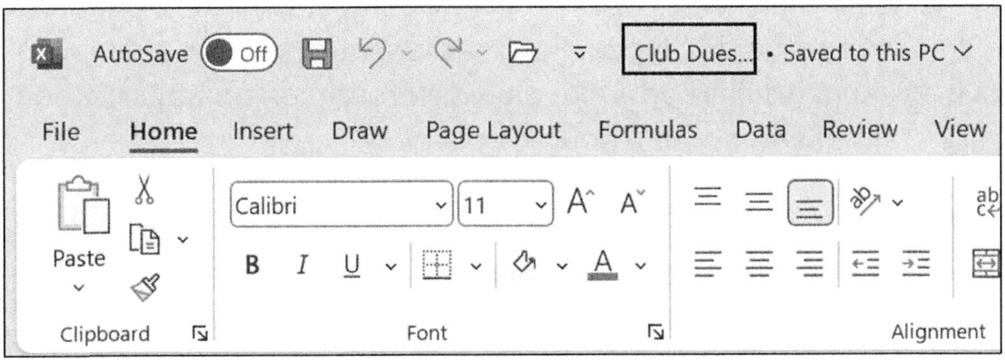

Figure 2.27

You might have noticed that there were other file types that you can save your Excel workbook as. If you click on the arrow next to Save as type, you will see a list of all the possible file types you can save your spreadsheet as (Figure 2.28).

Chapter 2 – Working with Excel

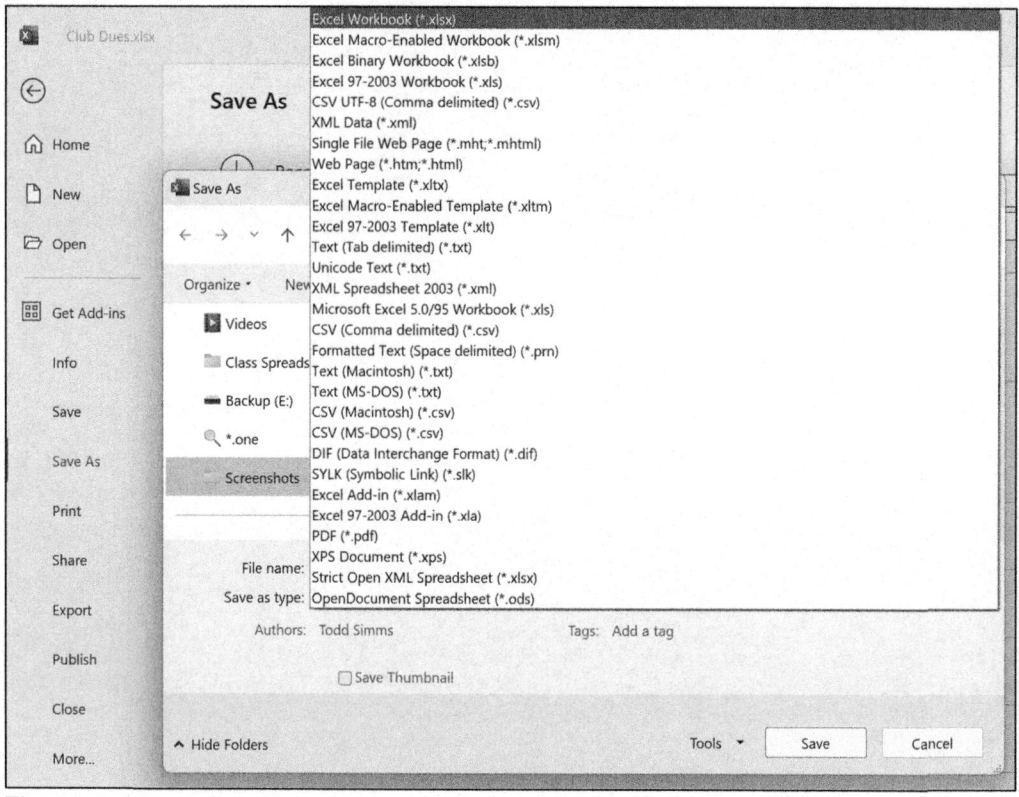

Figure 2.28

The default save type is an Excel Workbook (*xlsx) but you can also save it as an older version of Excel, web page, CSV file, text file as well as many other file types. For the most part, you probably won't have a reason to save your file as a different type unless someone requests that you do for a specific purpose.

Inserting Objects, Tables and Charts

There are many other things you can add to your Excel workbook besides text and numbers. If you go to the *Insert* tab, you can see that there are a variety of objects you can insert into your sheet. Many of these are beyond the scope of this book so I will only be covering the types that you will most likely be using until you become an Excel expert in the future.

Chapter 2 – Working with Excel

Tables

If you want to turn a range of data into a table, then you can simply highlight those cells with your mouse and click on *Table* from the Insert tab. Excel will then ask you to confirm the cells that will be in your table and also ask you if your table has headers which is a fancy word for titles.

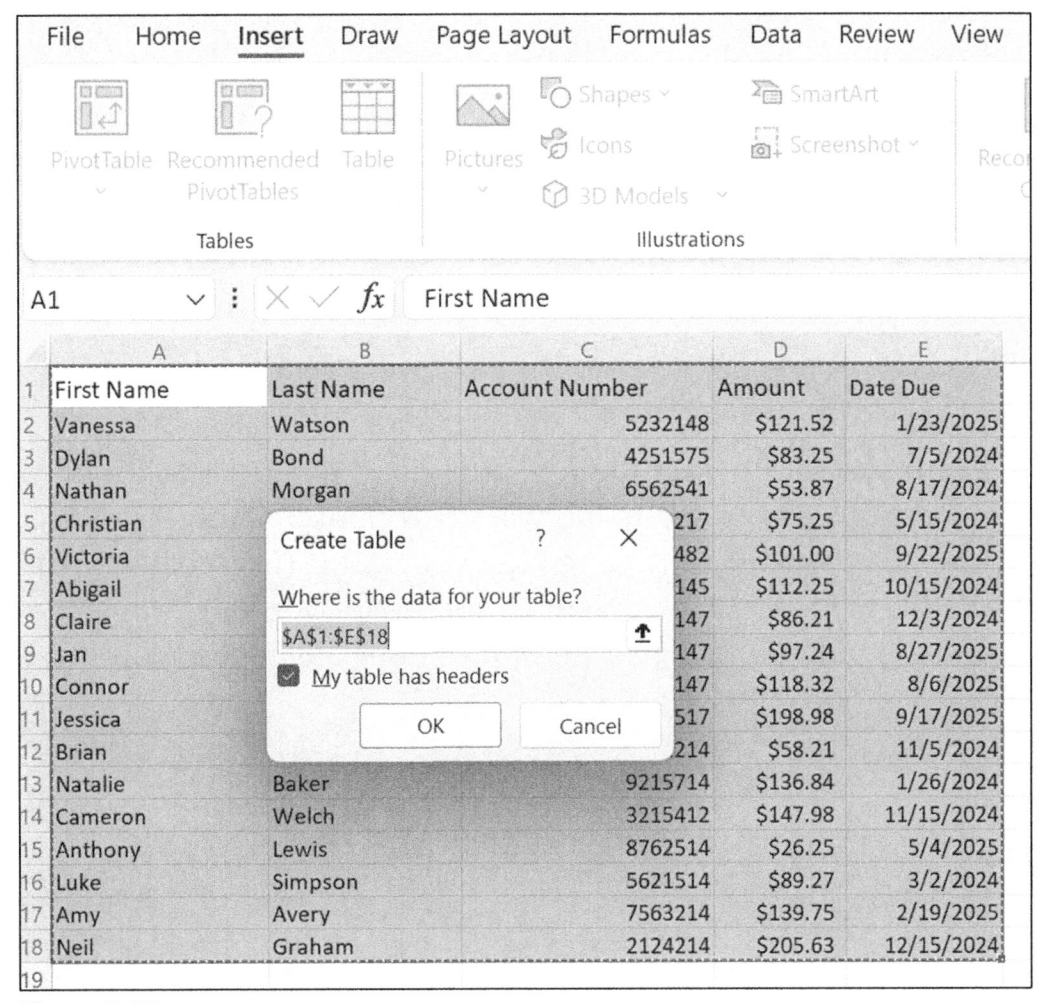

Figure 2.29

After you click OK, you will now see your data in table format with alternating colors for the rows.

45

Chapter 2 – Working with Excel

	A	B	C	D	E
1	First Name	Last Name	Account Number	Amount	Date Due
2	Vanessa	Watson	5232148	$121.52	1/23/2025
3	Dylan	Bond	4251575	$83.25	7/5/2024
4	Nathan	Morgan	6562541	$53.87	8/17/2024
5	Christian	Clarkson	4523217	$75.25	5/15/2024
6	Victoria	Dyer	4515482	$101.00	9/22/2025
7	Abigail	Randall	3625145	$112.25	10/15/2024
8	Claire	Ogden	3265147	$86.21	12/3/2024
9	Jan	Clark	9562147	$97.24	8/27/2025
10	Connor	Mathis	3265147	$118.32	8/6/2025
11	Jessica	McGrath	2233517	$198.98	9/17/2025
12	Brian	Randall	9532214	$58.21	11/5/2024
13	Natalie	Baker	9215714	$136.84	1/26/2024
14	Cameron	Welch	3215412	$147.98	11/15/2024
15	Anthony	Lewis	8762514	$26.25	5/4/2025
16	Luke	Simpson	5621514	$89.27	3/2/2024
17	Amy	Avery	7563214	$139.75	2/19/2025
18	Neil	Graham	2124214	$205.63	12/15/2024
19					

Figure 2.30

The top row will be your table headers and if you click the down arrow next to any of them you will get a popup screen similar to Figure 2.31 that you can use to filter your data. This that is beyond the scope of this book but might be something you will want to look into if you plan on using some of the more advanced features of Excel.

Chapter 2 – Working with Excel

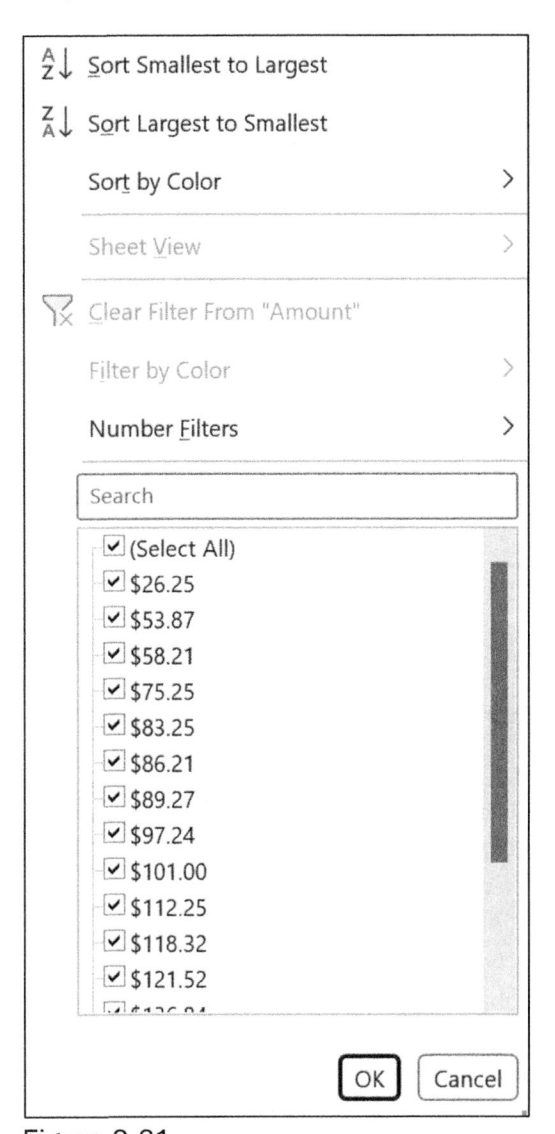

↓ Sort Smallest to Largest	
↓ Sort Largest to Smallest	
Sort by Color	>
Sheet View	>
⧩ Clear Filter From "Amount"	
Filter by Color	>
Number Filters	>
Search	
☑ (Select All) ☑ $26.25 ☑ $53.87 ☑ $58.21 ☑ $75.25 ☑ $83.25 ☑ $86.21 ☑ $89.27 ☑ $97.24 ☑ $101.00 ☑ $112.25 ☑ $118.32 ☑ $121.52 ☑ $136.84	
OK Cancel	

Figure 2.31

Pictures

You may find that you do not have a need to insert pictures into your spreadsheet compared to something like a Word document, but it's still one of the more common choices from the Insert tab so I figured I would mention it.

When you select the Pictures option, you will have three choices to choose from for your picture source. The first one is to choose an image that is stored on your hard drive. You can also choose the

Chapter 2 – Working with Excel

Stock Images choice which will let you search for images from the various categories as seen in Figure 2.32. One thing to note here is if you choose the Icons option, you will get the same choices as if you choose Icons from the same Illustrations group where you found Pictures.

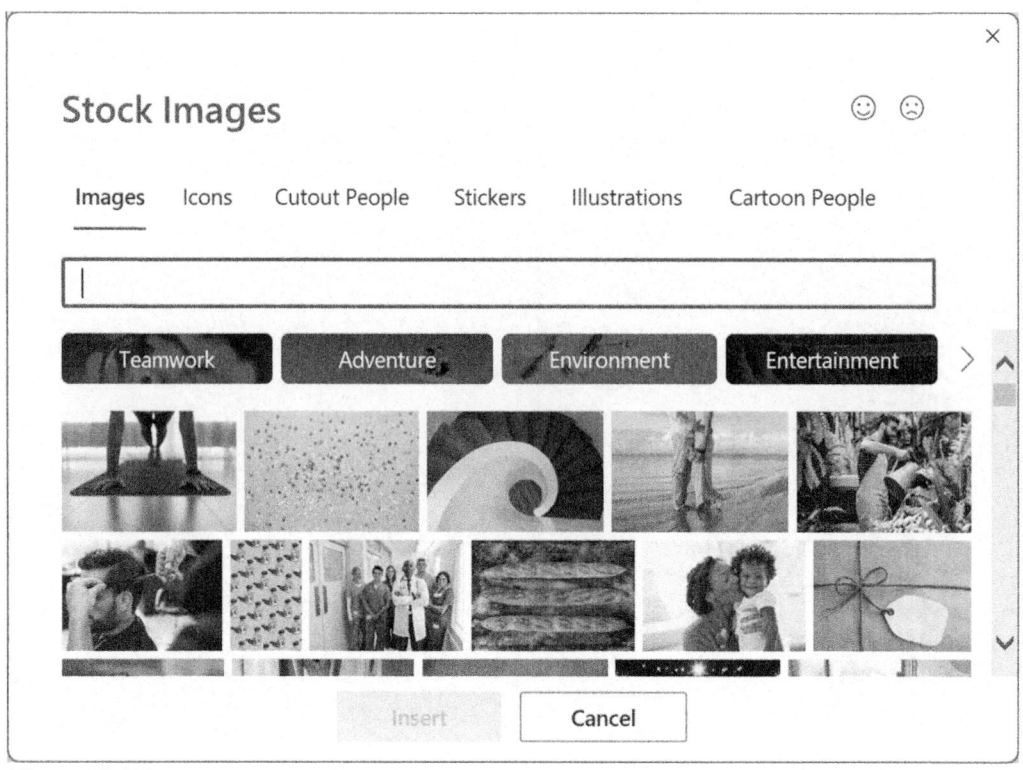

Figure 2.32

You can also use the *Online Images* choice to search the internet for any type of picture you can think of. If you leave the box checked that says *Creative Commons*, then you will only be shown results that are legal to use in your work. But if you are just adding images for personal use or for something at the office that will never make it to the public, you can leave this box unchecked to see additional images.

Chapter 2 – Working with Excel

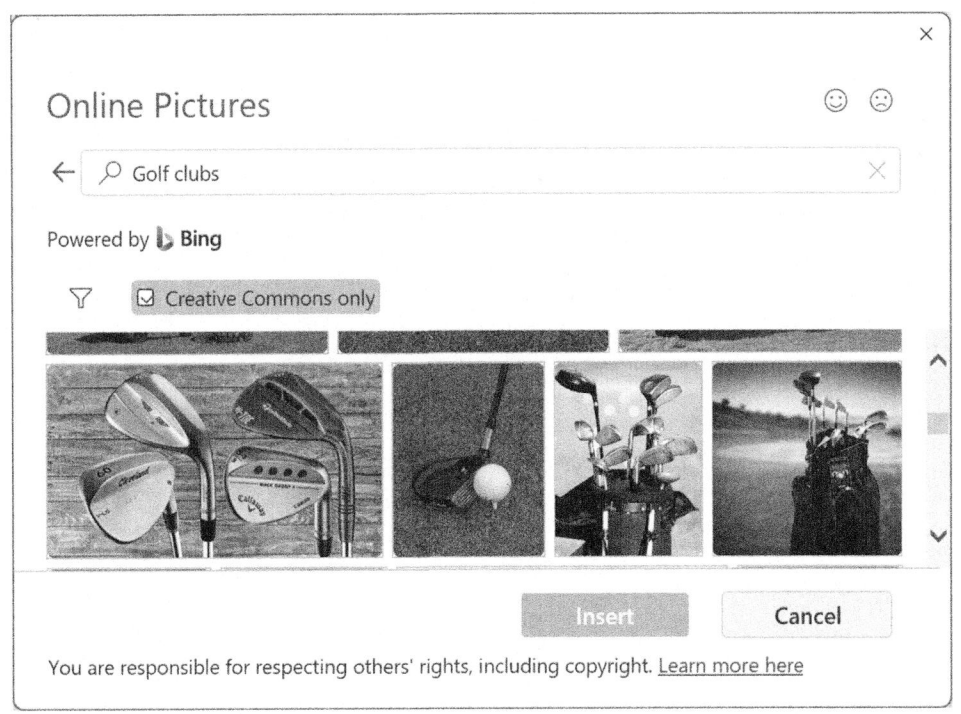

Figure 2.33

Once you have the image inserted into your spreadsheet, you can then move it wherever you like and resize it as needed.

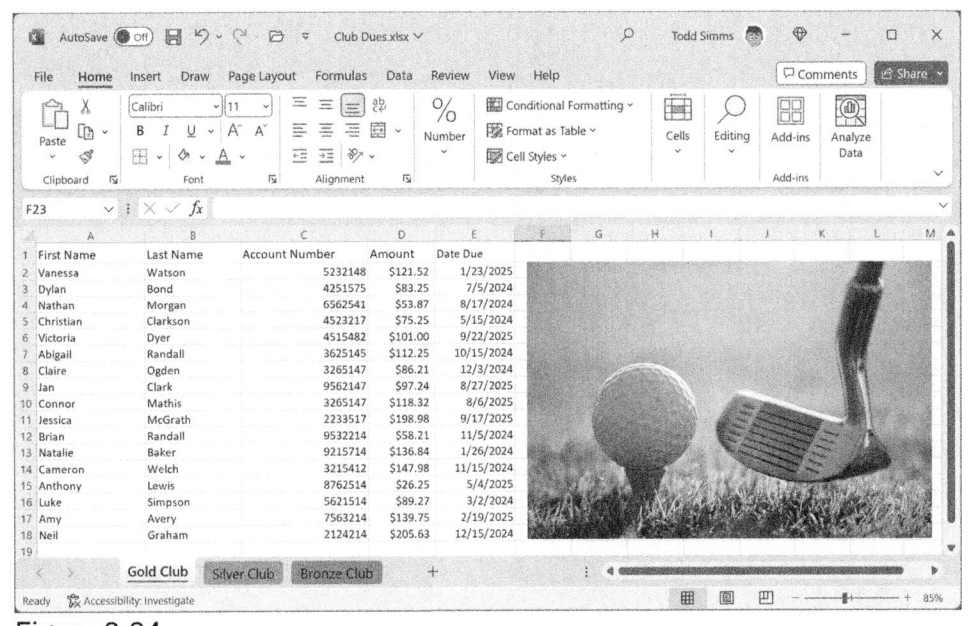

Figure 2.34

Chapter 2 – Working with Excel

Shapes

Shapes come in very handy because you can add them anywhere you like within your spreadsheet and also change their size, shape and color as needed. They are broken down into categories as seen in figure 2.35.

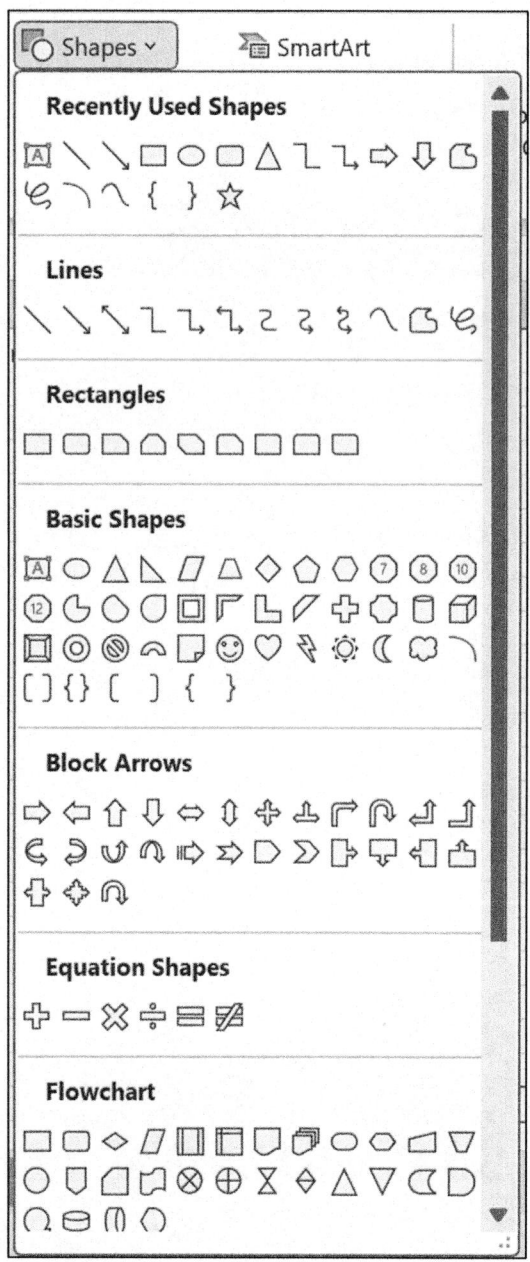

Figure 2.35

Chapter 2 – Working with Excel

Figure 2.36 shows some random shapes placed in my spreadsheet just to show you how they work.

	A	B	C	D	E
1	First Name	Last Name	Account Number	Amount	Date Due
2	Vanessa	Watson	5232148	$121.52	1/23/2025
3	Dylan	Bond	4251575	$83.25	7/5/2024
4	Nathan	Morgan	6562541	$53.87	8/17/2024
5	Christian	Clarkson	4523217	$75.25	5/15/2024
6	Victoria	Dyer	4515482	$101.00	9/22/2025
7	Abigail	Randall	3625145	$112.25	10/15/2024
8	Claire	Ogden	3265147	$86.21	12/3/2024
9	Jan	Clark	9562147	$97.24	8/27/2025
10	Connor	Mathis	3265147	$118.32	8/6/2025
11	Jessica	McGrath	2233517	$198.98	9/17/2025
12	Brian	Randall	9532214	$58.21	11/5/2024
13	Natalie	Baker	9215714	$136.84	1/26/2024
14	Cameron	Welch	3215412	$147.98	11/15/2024
15	Anthony	Lewis	8762514	$26.25	5/4/2025
16	Luke	Simpson	5621514	$89.27	3/2/2024
17	Amy	Avery	7563214	$120.75	2/19/2025
18	Neil	Graham	2124214		12/15/2024
19					

Figure 2.36

Charts

Inserting charts is a bit more of an advanced topic but I wanted to discuss it just in case you have a need to use them. You can have Excel create charts for you based on the data you select on your worksheet. Figure 2.37 shows that I have selected the *First Name*, *Last Name* and *Amount* columns for my data range.

Chapter 2 – Working with Excel

	A	B	C	D	E
1	First Name	Last Name	Account Number	Amount	Date Due
2	Vanessa	Watson	5232148	$121.52	1/23/2025
3	Dylan	Bond	4251575	$83.25	7/5/2024
4	Nathan	Morgan	6562541	$53.87	8/17/2024
5	Christian	Clarkson	4523217	$75.25	5/15/2024
6	Victoria	Dyer	4515482	$101.00	9/22/2025
7	Abigail	Randall	3625145	$112.25	10/15/2024
8	Claire	Ogden	3265147	$86.21	12/3/2024
9	Jan	Clark	9562147	$97.24	8/27/2025
10	Connor	Mathis	3265147	$118.32	8/6/2025
11	Jessica	McGrath	2233517	$198.98	9/17/2025
12	Brian	Randall	9532214	$58.21	11/5/2024
13	Natalie	Baker	9215714	$136.84	1/26/2024
14	Cameron	Welch	3215412	$147.98	11/15/2024
15	Anthony	Lewis	8762514	$26.25	5/4/2025
16	Luke	Simpson	5621514	$89.27	3/2/2024
17	Amy	Avery	7563214	$139.75	2/19/2025
18	Neil	Graham	2124214	$205.63	12/15/2024
19					

Figure 2.37

Once I have my data selected, I can click on one of the chart types from the *Charts* group or I can click on *Recommended Charts* which will show you the chart types that Excel recommends based on the type of data you have selected.

Chapter 2 – Working with Excel

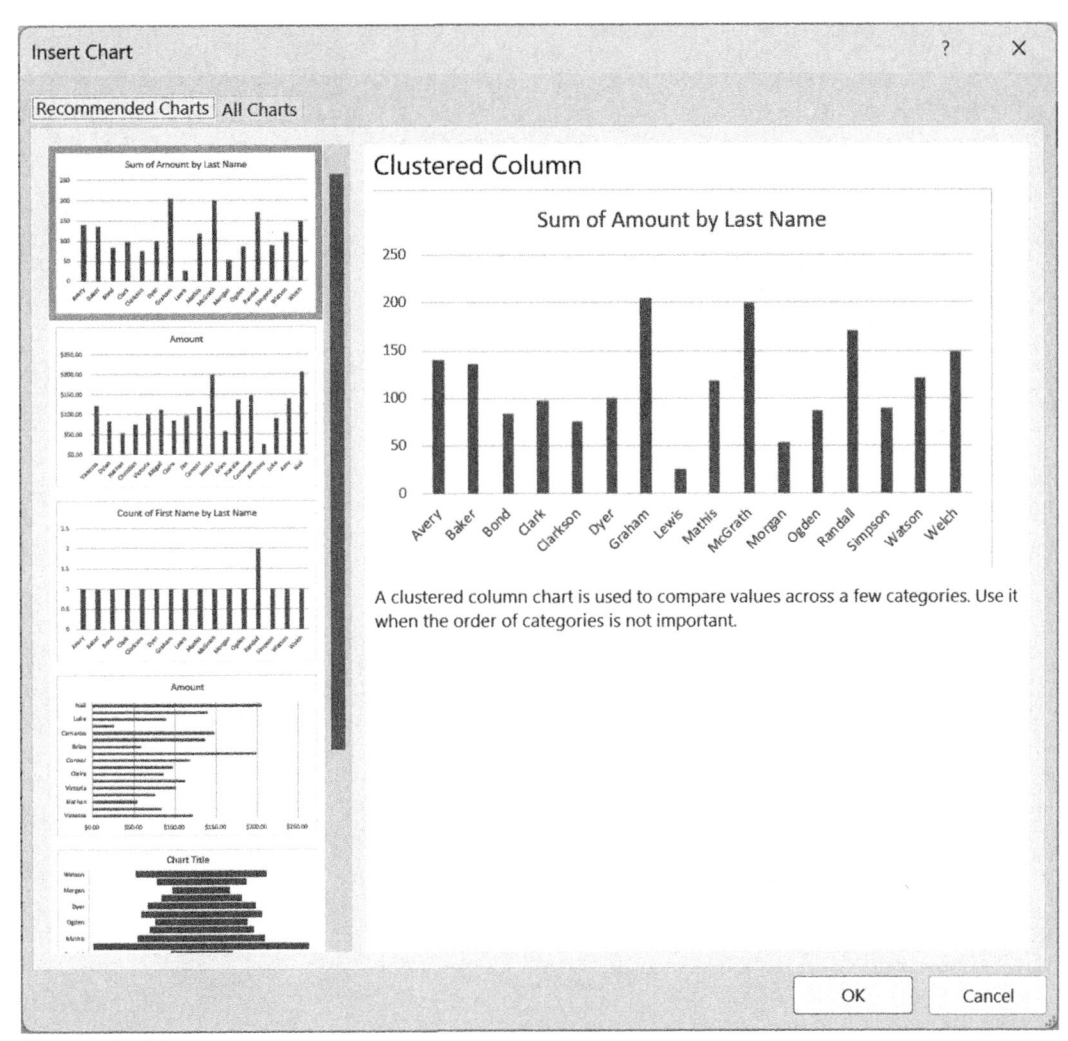

Figure 2.38

You can also click on *All Charts* to see the other chart types you can use. Just keep in mind that not every chart type will work well with all data types.

Chapter 2 – Working with Excel

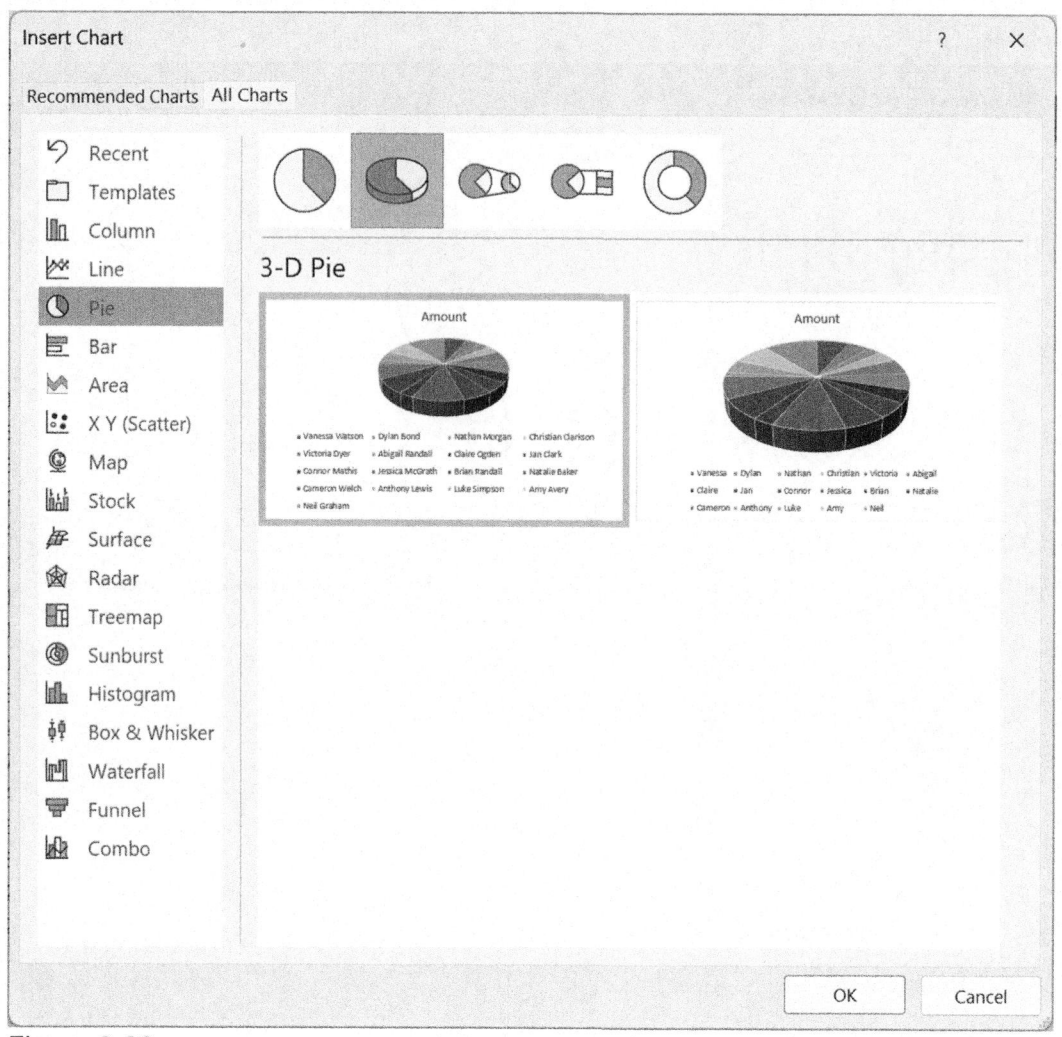

Figure 2.39

I will now select a column bar type chart from the recommended charts and Excel will then insert the chart into my spreadsheet as seen in Figure 2.40.

Chapter 2 – Working with Excel

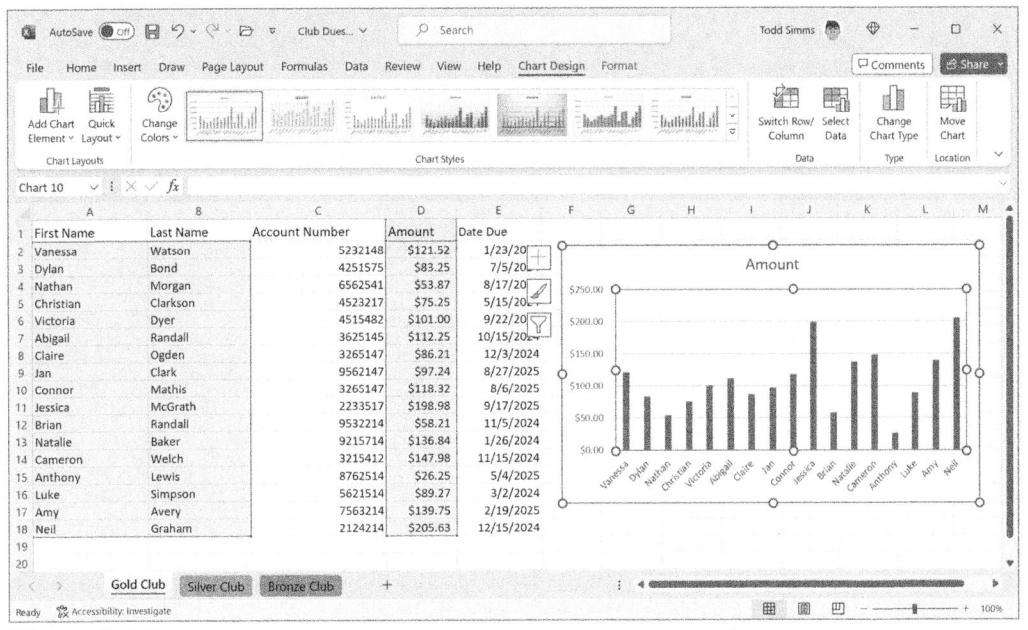

Figure 2.40

I can now move or resize the chart as needed and when I select it, I will see the *Chart Design* tab in the ribbon where I can customize the way it looks or what data is displayed within my chart. You will also notice how when you select your chart, it will highlight the data from your worksheet that is contained within the specific chart.

Links

Links are used to create a shortcut or pointer to another location such as a webpage or another Excel file for example. Then when the user clicks on the link, they will be taken to that location right from the spreadsheet itself.

In the example below, I have some text in a cell that says **Member Login Portal**. I will then select that cell and click on the *Link* button from the Ribbon, and I will have several choices as to what type of link I want to create for this text.

Chapter 2 – Working with Excel

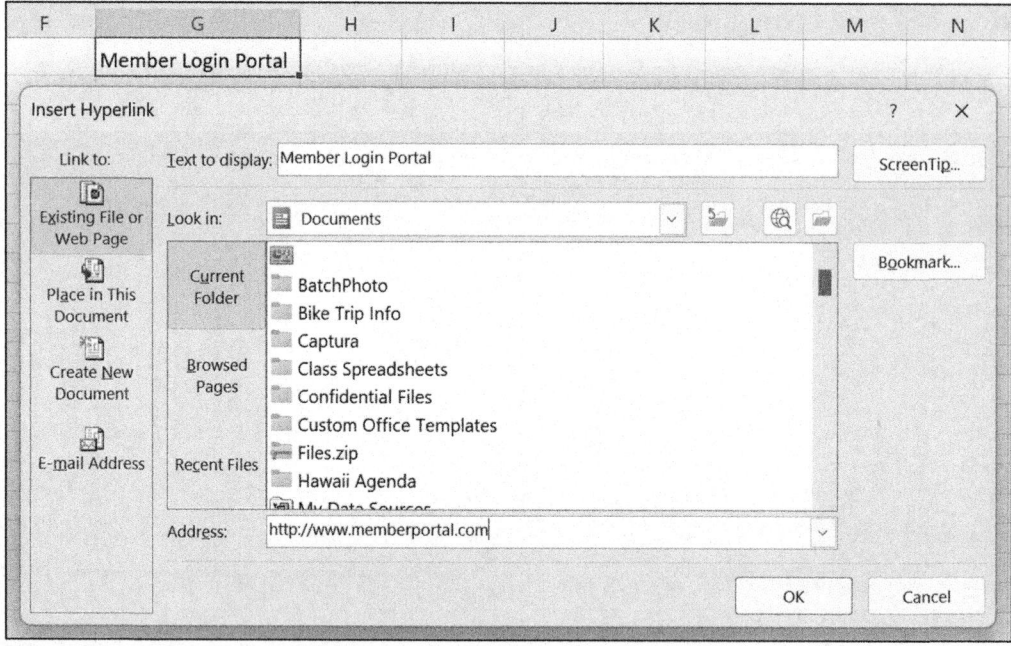

Figure 2.41

The first option lets you create a link to another file on your computer or to a website. You can also create a link that will take you to a specific location within your workbook such as a different worksheet altogether. If you want Excel to create a new spreadsheet and then create a link to it, you can do so using the *Create New Document* option. Finally, you can also create a link to an email address so when the user clicks on it, it will open their email app with the address filled in.

I will use the website option and type in the website address in the Address box as seen in Figure 2.42. After I click OK, the text in my cell will become blue and underlined, indicating it is a link. Then when someone clicks on it, their web browser will open and take them to that webpage. If I hover my mouse over the link, it will show me the website address associated with the link.

Chapter 2 – Working with Excel

G	H
Member Login Portal	

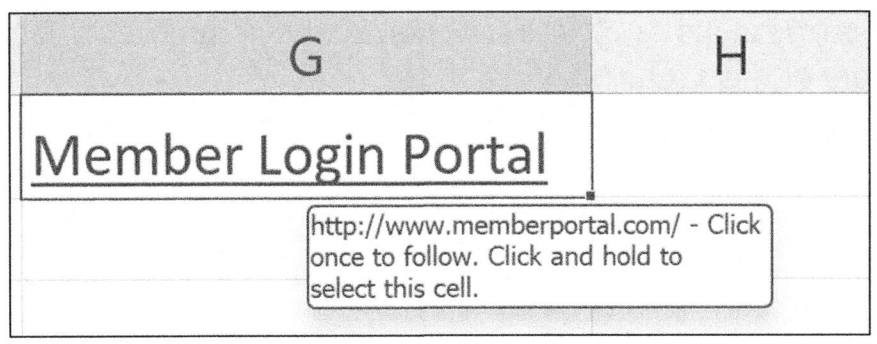

http://www.memberportal.com/ - Click once to follow. Click and hold to select this cell.

Figure 2.42

Comments

If you plan on sharing your Excel spreadsheet with other people, then you can add comments to cells to make others aware of things that might need to be changed or things that you want others to do on your spreadsheet. They can then reply to your comments and add their own.

To leave a comment, simply select the cell you want it to apply to and then click the *Comment* button on the Ribbon. Then you can type in your comment and click the paper airplane button or press Ctrl-Enter to post it.

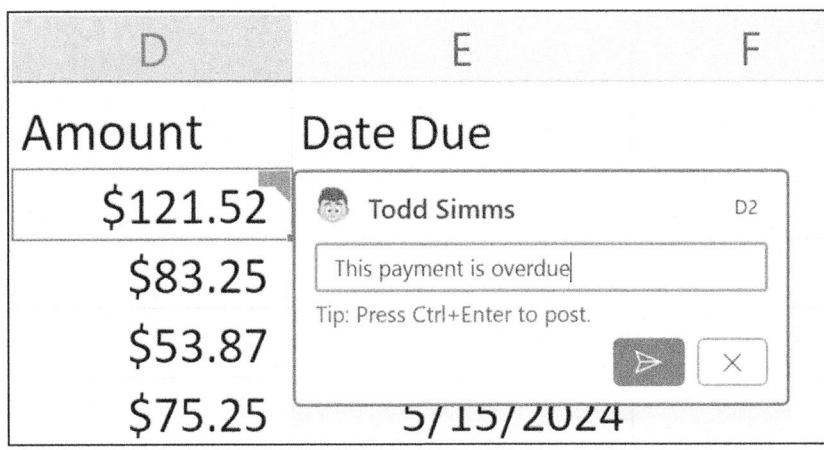

D	E	F
Amount	Date Due	
$121.52	Todd Simms	D2
$83.25	This payment is overdue	
$53.87	Tip: Press Ctrl+Enter to post.	
$75.25	5/15/2024	

Figure 2.43

Then when someone else opens your spreadsheet and clicks on that cell, they will see your comment and be able to reply if needed.

Chapter 2 – Working with Excel

If you click on the ellipsis (...), you can then do things such as delete the comment or mark it as resolved.

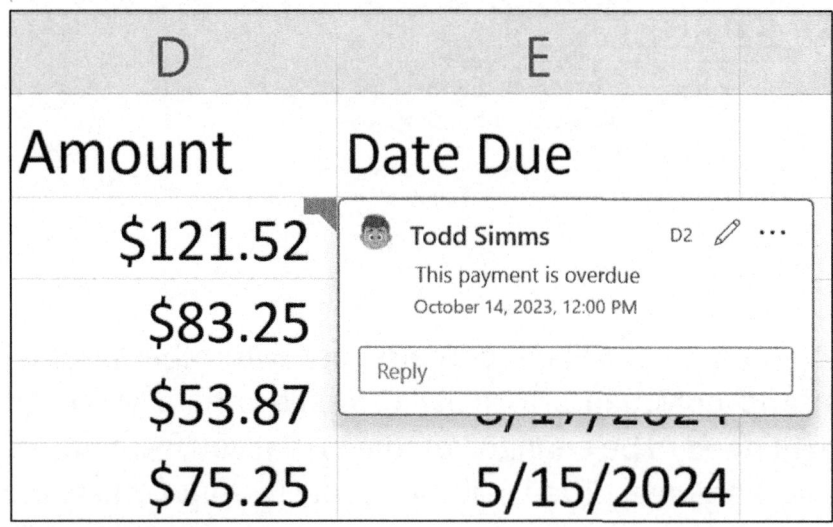

Figure 2.44

Text

The Text section in the Insert tab has several tools that you can use to add text related objects to your spreadsheet.

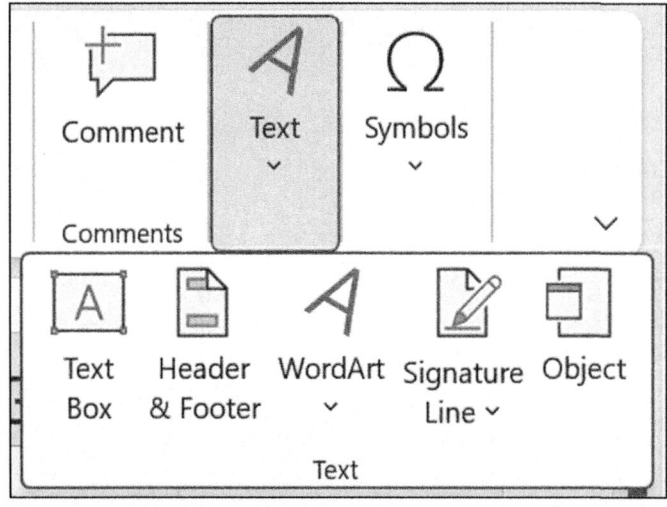

Figure 2.45

Chapter 2 – Working with Excel

Here is a breakdown of the tools from the Text section.

- **Text Box** – If you need to add some text to your worksheet but do not want it to be contained in a cell, you can add a standalone text box that you can then move around your worksheet as needed. You can then change the color of the text box and format the text just like any other text.

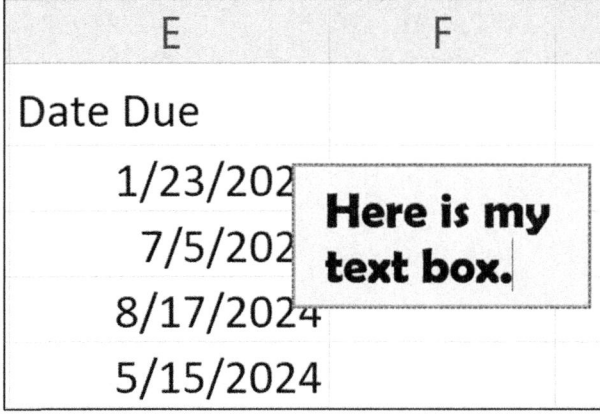

Figure 2.46

- **Header & Footer** – Excel allows you to add text to the header and footer sections of your worksheet just like you can do with Word documents.

- **Word Art** – Word Art is similar to adding a text box except you have some built in styles that you can apply to your text to make them stand out.

Figure 2.47

Chapter 2 – Working with Excel

- **Signature Line** – If you need to have a sheet in your workbook digitally signed, you can insert a signature line. You can fill in some of the information for the signature before applying it to your worksheet. Then once you add the signature line, you can move it around the sheet as needed. Just keep in mind that for someone to be able to digitally sign your sheet, you will need a digital ID configured.

Figure 2.48

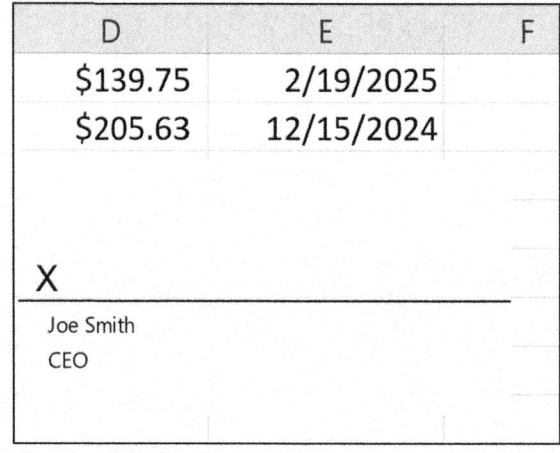

D	E	F
$139.75	2/19/2025	
$205.63	12/15/2024	

X_____
Joe Smith
CEO

Figure 2.49

Chapter 2 – Working with Excel

- **Object** – If you need to insert another file or link to a file then you can do so from the Object section. You can either insert the file so you can see the pages on your spreadsheet or link to the file so that when they click the icon, it will open the file using its default app. I prefer the link method using the display as icon feature because it's much cleaner appearing on your worksheet as seen in figure 2.50.

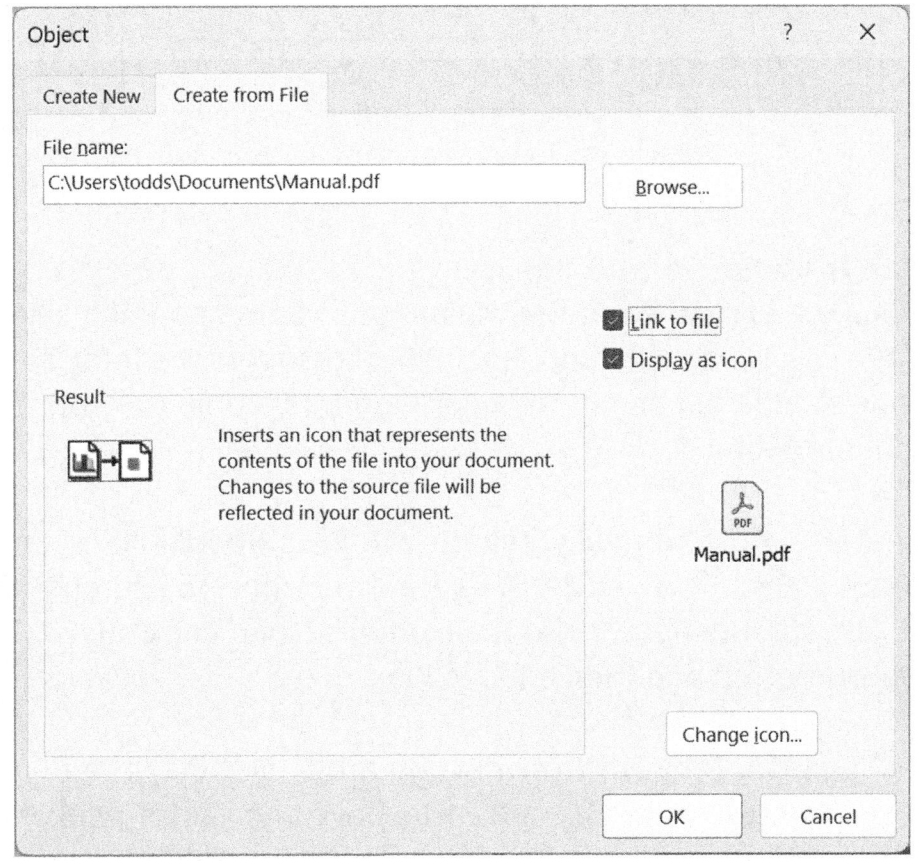

Figure 2.50

Chapter 2 – Working with Excel

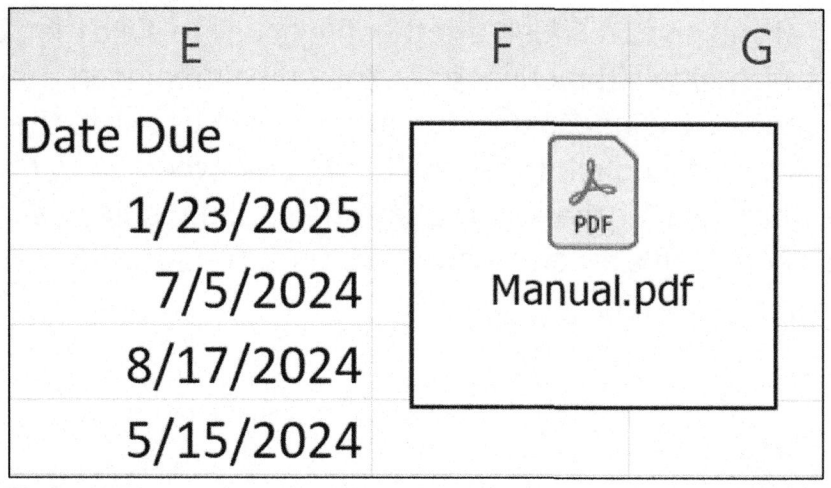

	E	F	G
	Date Due		
	1/23/2025		
	7/5/2024	Manual.pdf	
	8/17/2024		
	5/15/2024		

Figure 2.51

Search Options
If you have a spreadsheet that has a lot of data spanning several rows and columns, you might find it hard to locate the information that you need, especially if your workbook contains multiple worksheets within it.

Fortunately, you can easily search within a worksheet or entire workbook in Excel to find what you are looking for. To search within your Excel spreadsheet, go to the Home tab and click on the *Find and Select* button and then choose *Find*.

In the *Find what* box, type in what you are searching for and then you can click the *Find All* button to have the entire worksheet searched and have the results shown in the box below as seen in Figure 2.52. You can then click on any of the results to be taken to that cell in your worksheet. If you click the *Find Next* button, you will be shown each instance of the search results one at a time.

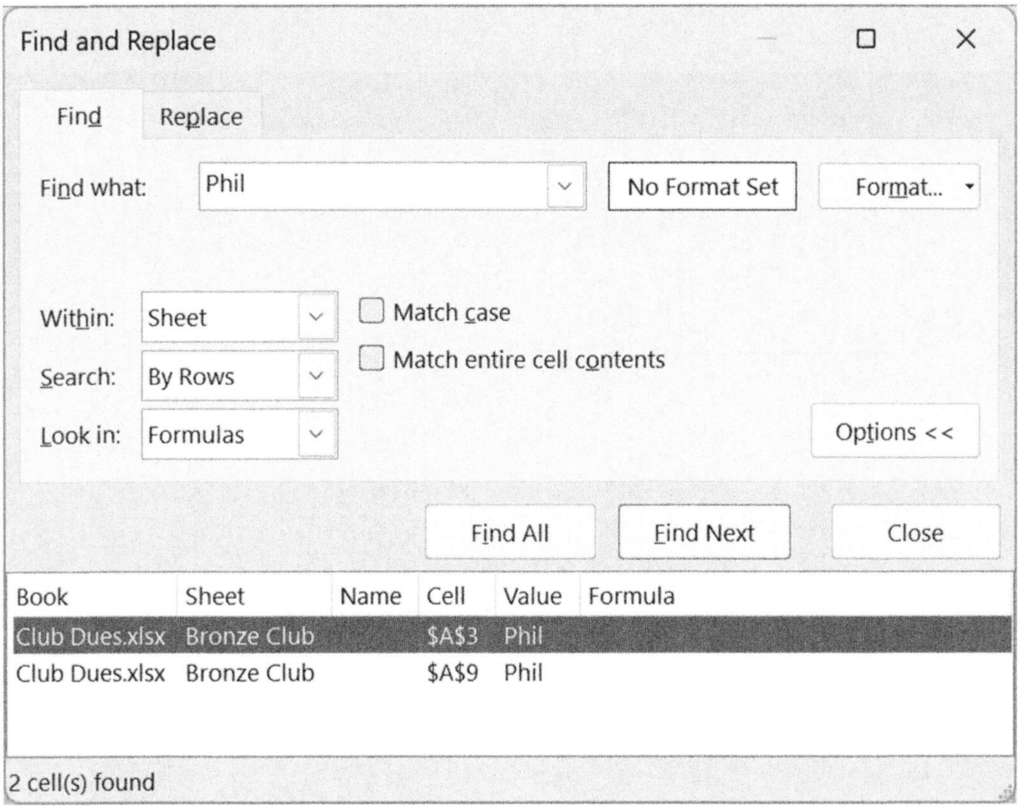

Chapter 2 – Working with Excel

Figure 2.52

If you change the search from *Sheet* to *Workbook* from the *Within* dropdown, Excel will search all the worksheets within your file and show you the results all in one place. As you can see in Figure 2.53, there are now three results for Phil since one of them is in a different worksheet.

Chapter 2 – Working with Excel

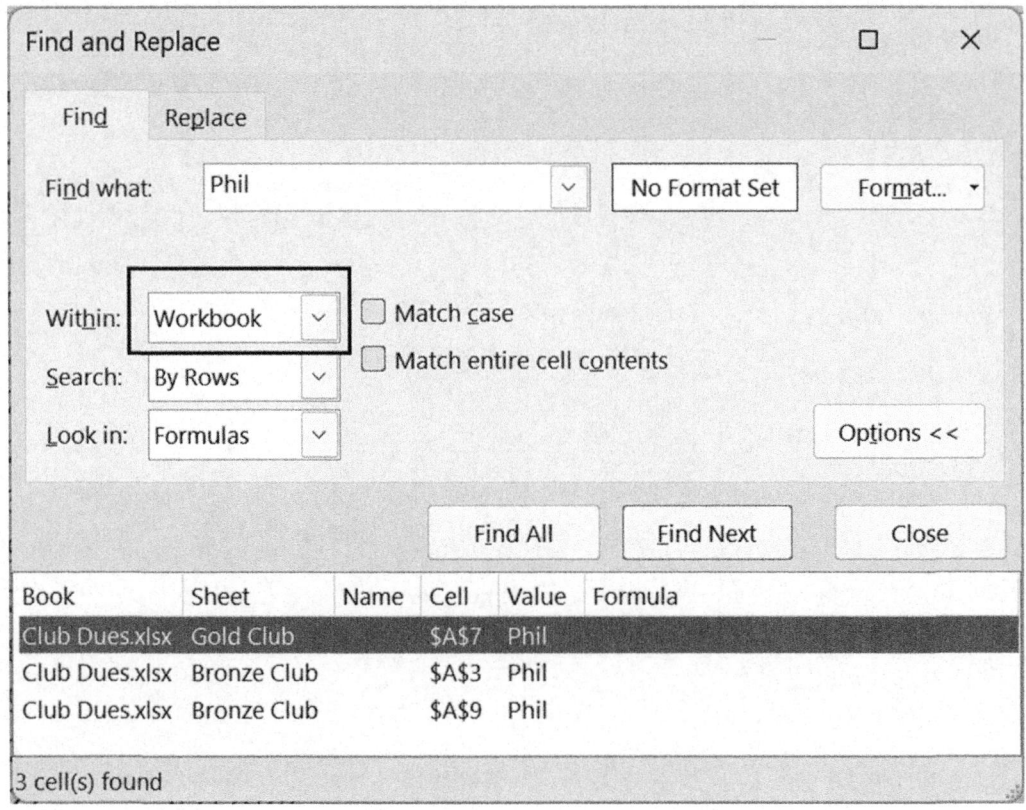

Figure 2.53

One nice feature that Excel has that you can access from the search options is the ability to replace multiple instances of text or numbers with different text or numbers, so you do not need to do it manually.

From the same Find and Replace box, click on the *Replace* tab and you will then be able to specify what you wish to have replaced and with what you wish to replace it with.

Figure 2.54 shows that I want to replace the name Phil with Philip and if I were to click the *Replace* button, it would show me each instance of the name Phil that it can replace one at a time and I can choose to replace the name with Philip or leave it as Phil.

Chapter 2 – Working with Excel

If I click the *Replace All* button, Excel will then replace all instances of Phil with Philip in the current worksheet. If I change the setting to Workbook, then it will change the name in all my worksheets.

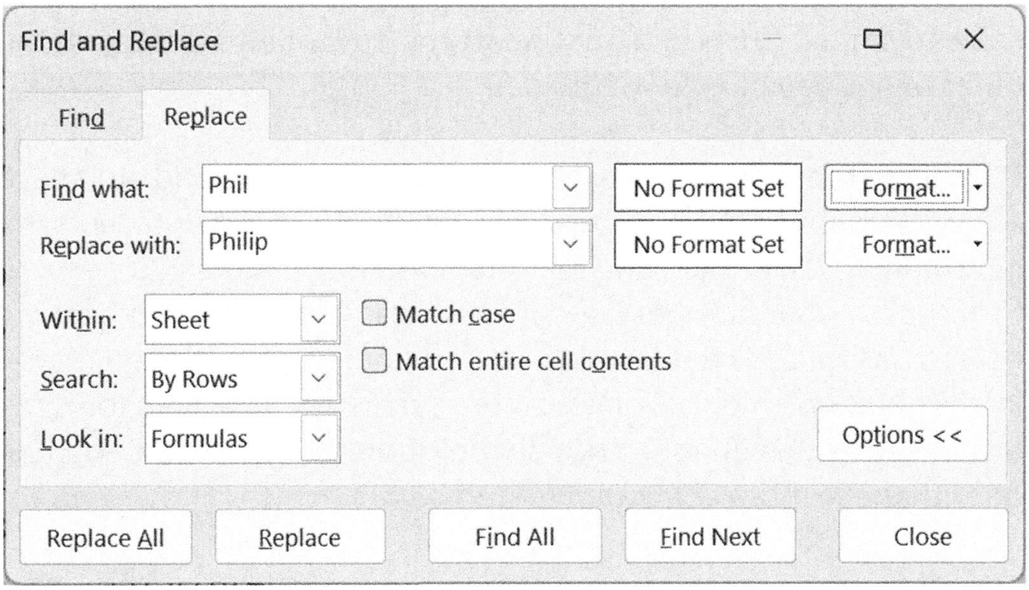

Figure 2.54

Chapter 3 – Functions, Formulas and Sorting

Now that I have some data in my spreadsheet, it's time to get into some of the more advanced features of Microsoft Excel. But when I say advanced, this is still not nearly as advanced as many of the other things you can do with Excel!

One of the reasons to use Excel is to store your data and also have a way to manipulate it to help you analyze it in order to find the information you are looking for. There are many tools you can use to "crunch" your numbers and in this chapter, I will be discussing how to use functions, formulas and sorting. As I mentioned earlier in this book, you may never have the need to use any of the features discussed in this chapter, but it won't hurt to know what you can do with these more advanced features.

Functions
If you have been using Excel for any amount of time, you have probably heard the term formulas being used to describe a way to work with your data to do things such as perform mathematical calculations etc.

Functions are used in the same way, but you can think of them as preconfigured formulas that you simply apply to your data without having to create them yourself. If you go to the *Home* tab and then the *Editing* group, you will see what is known as the auto sum symbol (Σ), and if you click on it, you will be shown the most common Excel functions that you can apply to your data.

Chapter 3 – Functions, Formulas and Filters

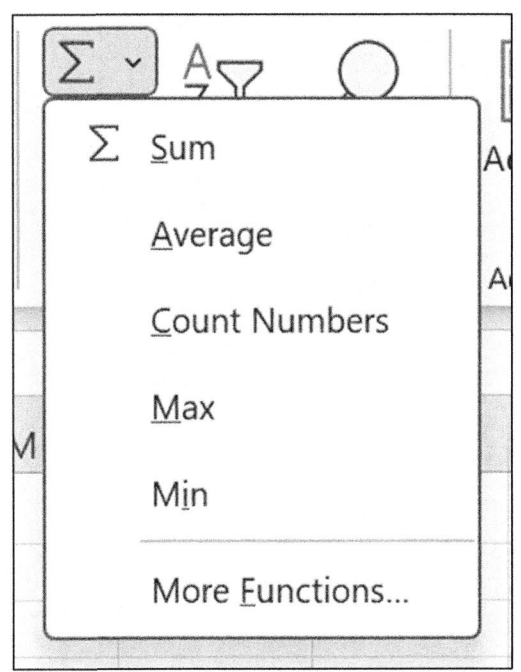

Figure 3.1

If you click on *More Functions*, you will be shown all the other available functions broken down into categories. You can also search for a function by typing a brief description of what you are looking to do (figure 3.2).

Chapter 3 – Functions, Formulas and Filters

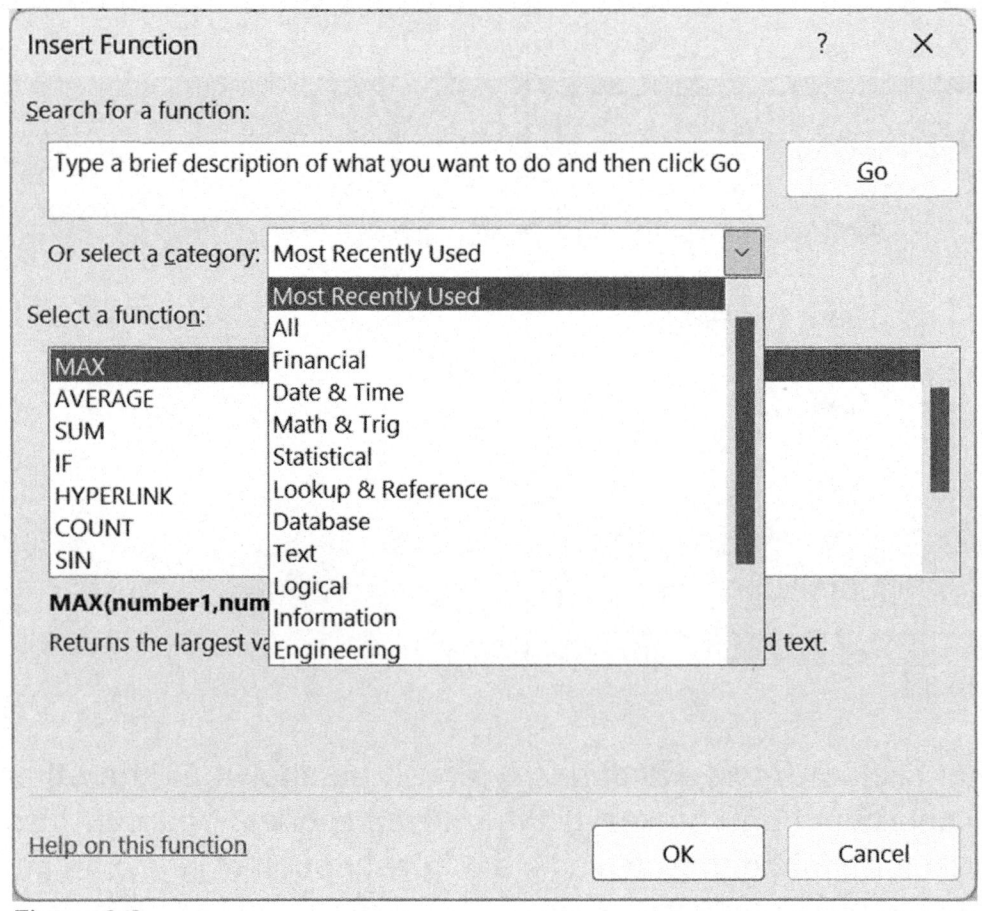

Figure 3.2

For my example, I want to add up all the dollar amounts from my D column and have the total be placed at the end of the column itself. To do this, I will select the data that I want to have added up and then leave an empty cell at the bottom for the total as seen in Figure 3.3.

Chapter 3 – Functions, Formulas and Filters

	A	B	C	D	E
4	Nathan	Morgan	6562541	$53.87	8/17/2024
5	Christian	Clarkson	4523217	$75.25	5/15/2024
6	Victoria	Dyer	4515482	$101.00	9/22/2025
7	Phil	Randall	3625145	$112.25	10/15/2024
8	Claire	Ogden	3265147	$86.21	12/3/2024
9	Jan	Clark	9562147	$97.24	8/27/2025
10	Connor	Mathis	3265147	$118.32	8/6/2025
11	Jessica	McGrath	2233517	$198.98	9/17/2025
12	Brian	Randall	9532214	$58.21	11/5/2024
13	Natalie	Baker	9215714	$136.84	1/26/2024
14	Cameron	Welch	3215412	$147.98	11/15/2024
15	Anthony	Lewis	8762514	$26.25	5/4/2025
16	Luke	Simpson	5621514	$89.27	3/2/2024
17	Amy	Avery	7563214	$139.75	2/19/2025
18	Neil	Graham	2124214	$205.63	12/15/2024
19					
20	Total				

Figure 3.3

Now when I click on the auto sum icon, the values in the selected cells will be added together and I will now have the total displayed below them.

Chapter 3 – Functions, Formulas and Filters

D
$53.87
$75.25
$101.00
$112.25
$86.21
$97.24
$118.32
$198.98
$58.21
$136.84
$147.98
$26.25
$89.27
$139.75
$205.63
$1,647.05

Figure 3.4

If I were to change a value in one or more of the cells, my total would automatically be changed to reflect the changes. I can even move the cell with the total down to make room for new data and it will still add up everything in that column.

Now let's say I wanted the average dollar amount owed and want to have that number be located in a cell in a completely different column. To do so, I can click in the cell where I want my average

Chapter 3 – Functions, Formulas and Filters

value to be and then select the *Average* function and then use my mouse to select the dollar amount range as seen in Figure 3.5. As you can see, Excel is taking the average of cells D4 through D18 and will change as I select or deselect cells.

D	E	F	G	H
$75.25	5/15/2024			
$101.00	9/22/2025			
$112.25	10/15/2024			
$86.21	12/3/2024			
$97.24	8/27/2025			
$118.32	8/6/2025			
$198.98	9/17/2025			
$58.21	11/5/2024			
$136.84	1/26/2024			
$147.98	11/15/2024			
$26.25	5/4/2025			
$89.27	3/2/2024			
$139.75	2/19/2025			
$205.63	12/15/2024			
$1,647.05		=AVERAGE(D5:D18)		
		AVERAGE(**number1**, [number2], ...)		

Figure 3.5

When I press Enter on my keyboard, I will now see that the average value of all these cells is $109.80.

Chapter 3 – Functions, Formulas and Filters

D	E	F
$75.25	5/15/2024	
$101.00	9/22/2025	
$112.25	10/15/2024	
$86.21	12/3/2024	
$97.24	8/27/2025	
$118.32	8/6/2025	
$198.98	9/17/2025	
$58.21	11/5/2024	
$136.84	1/26/2024	
$147.98	11/15/2024	
$26.25	5/4/2025	
$89.27	3/2/2024	
$139.75	2/19/2025	
$205.63	12/15/2024	
$1,647.05		$109.80

Figure 3.6

The Formula Bar

As you have been adding data to cells, you might have noticed that when you click on a particular cell, you can see that same value in the box at the top of the worksheet. Even though this box is called the formula bar, it doesn't mean that it is only used for formulas.

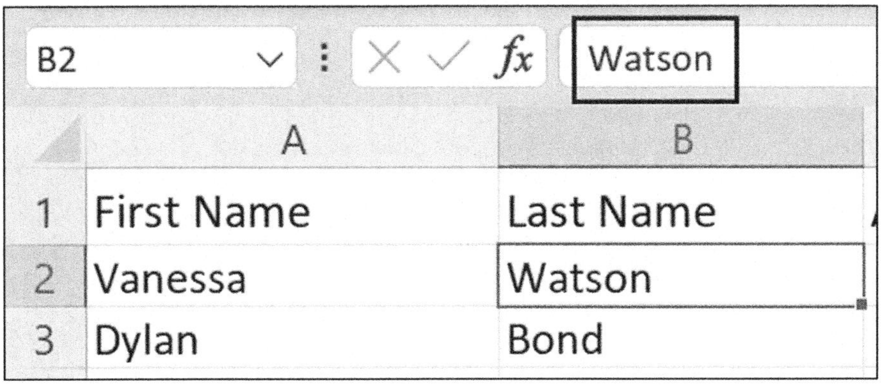

Chapter 3 – Functions, Formulas and Filters

	A	B
1	First Name	Last Name
2	Vanessa	Watson
3	Dylan	Bond

(B2 = Watson)

Figure 3.7

You can actually type or even paste data into the formula bar and whichever cell is selected will then contain that data. It's a great way to paste in data and not include any formatting such as bold text or fancy fonts because the formatting will be removed from that text when pasted into the formula bar.

The formula bar can however be used to create and view formulas contained within cells in your worksheet. If I were to select the total value in column D that I have after using the auto sum function discussed in the last section, the formula used to create that function value would be shown in the formula bar (Figure 3.8).

As you can see, the value of $1647.05 was obtained by taking the sum of cells D4 through D19. You can even edit the formula in the formula bar as needed. Let's say you didn't want to include the amounts in any cell after D15, you can simply change the formula to read =SUM(D4:D15).

Chapter 3 – Functions, Formulas and Filters

	A	B	C	D
	D20		fx	=SUM(D4:D19)
1	First Name	Last Name	Account Number	Amount
2	Vanessa	Watson	5232148	$121.52
3	Dylan	Bond	4251575	$83.25
4	Nathan	Morgan	6562541	$53.87
5	Christian	Clarkson	4523217	$75.25
6	Victoria	Dyer	4515482	$101.00
7	Phil	Randall	3625145	$112.25
8	Claire	Ogden	3265147	$86.21
9	Jan	Clark	9562147	$97.24
10	Connor	Mathis	3265147	$118.32
11	Jessica	McGrath	2233517	$198.98
12	Brian	Randall	9532214	$58.21
13	Natalie	Baker	9215714	$136.84
14	Cameron	Welch	3215412	$147.98
15	Anthony	Lewis	8762514	$26.25
16	Luke	Simpson	5621514	$89.27
17	Amy	Avery	7563214	$139.75
18	Neil	Graham	2124214	$205.63
19				
20	Total			$1,647.05

Figure 3.8

We will be using the formula bar to a greater extent in the next section on creating formulas themselves.

One thing to take note of is that the formula bar will only show the contents of one cell at a time. So, if you were to select multiple cells by clicking on one cell, holding down the Shift key and clicking on another cell, the value in the formula bar would be that of the first cell you selected (Figure 3.9). If you used the Ctrl key method, then it would contain the value of the last cell you selected (Figure 3.10).

Chapter 3 – Functions, Formulas and Filters

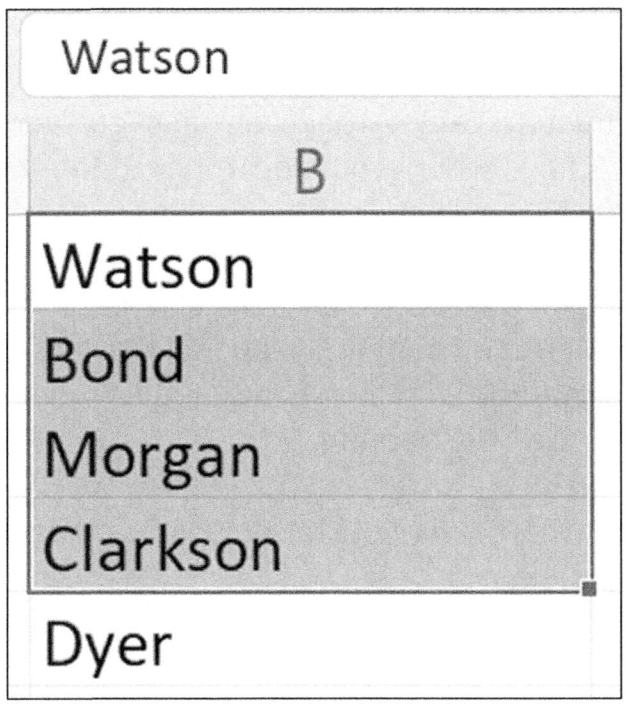

Figure 3.9

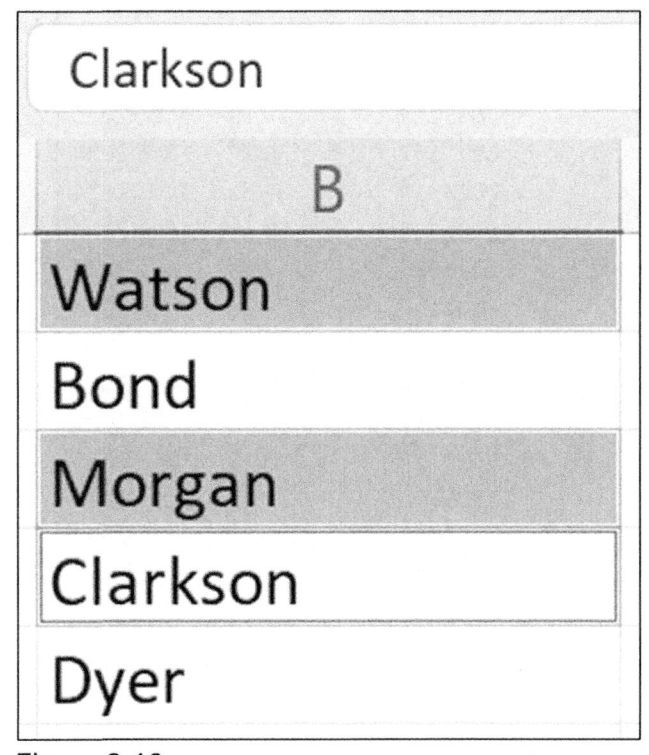

Figure 3.10

Chapter 3 – Functions, Formulas and Filters

Creating Formulas

Formulas are similar to functions, but they are created manually and can be much more customizable. They can also get very complex and difficult to follow when you add many different calculations to a single formula.

Of course, you can also create simple formulas if needed so for my first example, I will manually create a formula to add all the values in my D column using a different worksheet rather than use a function like I showed you in the prior section.

To begin, I will select the cell where I want the formula to be placed. So, in this case it will be cell D19.

	A	B	C	D	E
1	First Name	Last Name	Account Number	Amount	Date Due
2	Nathan	Pullman	5623147	115.25	5/23/2025
3	Phil	Thomson	3201201	75.23	3/14/2024
4	Christian	Churchill	2035214	115.32	9/17/2025
5	Audrey	Wallace	6920147	68.74	2/22/2024
6	Penelope	Churchill	2623014	201.51	4/15/2024
7	Mary	Fraser	9201424	89.65	4/13/2025
8	Rachel	Ince	8326210	113.24	8/7/2025
9	Phil	Bailey	2102157	79.34	9/3/2024
10	Heather	Kerr	8523624	92.54	1/25/2025
11	Theresa	Tucker	1230254	121.14	3/15/2024
12	Jack	McGrath	4236251	88.61	6/4/2025
13	Joshua	Roberts	5320214	145.21	12/2/2025
14	Alan	Peake	8236501	98.65	10/14/2024
15	Maria	Cortez	2362411	-25	9/15/2024
16	Kim	Lee	5124715	226.25	11/25/2025
17	Danny	Burke	8652147	-35.22	1/2/2024
18					
19					

Figure 3.11

Chapter 3 – Functions, Formulas and Filters

Next, I will begin typing my formula in the formula bar and will begin the process by typing an equal sign (=) indicating to Excel that this will be a formula and not just plain text or a number. I will then use the SUM function to indicate that I want to add the values that I will be entering next. I now have **=SUM** in my formula bar. Next, I will need to add an open parenthesis to tell the function what data to take action on.

Within the parenthesis I will then add the cell references that will be used for the calculation. So in this case it will be D2:D17 indicating cells D2 through and including D17. Finally, I will close the parenthesis to tell Excel only to act on this data range so my final formula will look like **=SUM(D2:D17)**. Then when I press the Enter key on my keyboard, the formula will be applied to that cell, and I will get a total of **1570.46**.

	A	B	C	D	E
1	First Name	Last Name	Account Number	Amount	Date Due
2	Nathan	Pullman	5623147	115.25	5/23/2025
3	Phil	Thomson	3201201	75.23	3/14/2024
4	Christian	Churchill	2035214	115.32	9/17/2025
5	Audrey	Wallace	6920147	68.74	2/22/2024
6	Penelope	Churchill	2623014	201.51	4/15/2024
7	Mary	Fraser	9201424	89.65	4/13/2025
8	Rachel	Ince	8326210	113.24	8/7/2025
9	Phil	Bailey	2102157	79.34	9/3/2024
10	Heather	Kerr	8523624	92.54	1/25/2025
11	Theresa	Tucker	1230254	121.14	3/15/2024
12	Jack	McGrath	4236251	88.61	6/4/2025
13	Joshua	Roberts	5320214	145.21	12/2/2025
14	Alan	Peake	8236501	98.65	10/14/2024
15	Maria	Cortez	2362411	-25	9/15/2024
16	Kim	Lee	5124715	226.25	11/25/2025
17	Danny	Burke	8652147	-35.22	1/2/2024
18					
19				1570.46	

Figure 3.12

Chapter 3 – Functions, Formulas and Filters

Now let's say I had a couple of members with some extra fees that I want to add to my total due value in cell D19 (Figure 3.13).

D	E	F
Amount	Date Due	Extra Fees
115.25	5/23/2025	
75.23	3/14/2024	
115.32	9/17/2025	
68.74	2/22/2024	15.47
201.51	4/15/2024	
89.65	4/13/2025	
113.24	8/7/2025	10.52
79.34	9/3/2024	
92.54	1/25/2025	
121.14	3/15/2024	
88.61	6/4/2025	
145.21	12/2/2025	
98.65	10/14/2024	
-25	9/15/2024	
226.25	11/25/2025	
-35.22	1/2/2024	
1570.46		

Figure 3.13

I can simply edit my formula to add these additional fees to my total by clicking in the formula bar and adding cells F5 and F8 to my current formula (Figure 3.14). All I need to do is add the + symbol

Chapter 3 – Functions, Formulas and Filters

for add and then type in (or click on) the cells with the data to have them added to my total which is shown in Figure 3.15.

=SUM(D2:D17)+F5+F8			
C	D	E	F
ccount Number	Amount	Date Due	Extra Fees
5623147	115.25	5/23/2025	
3201201	75.23	3/14/2024	
2035214	115.32	9/17/2025	
6920147	68.74	2/22/2024	15.47
2623014	201.51	4/15/2024	
9201424	89.65	4/13/2025	
8326210	113.24	8/7/2025	10.52
2102157	79.34	9/3/2024	
8523624	92.54	1/25/2025	
1230254	121.14	3/15/2024	
4236251	88.61	6/4/2025	
5320214	145.21	12/2/2025	
8236501	98.65	10/14/2024	
2362411	-25	9/15/2024	
5124715	226.25	11/25/2025	
8652147	-35.22	1/2/2024	
	D17)+F5+F8		

Figure 3.14

Chapter 3 – Functions, Formulas and Filters

=SUM(D2:D17)+F5+F8			
C	D	E	F
ccount Number	Amount	Date Due	Extra Fees
5623147	115.25	5/23/2025	
3201201	75.23	3/14/2024	
2035214	115.32	9/17/2025	
6920147	68.74	2/22/2024	15.47
2623014	201.51	4/15/2024	
9201424	89.65	4/13/2025	
8326210	113.24	8/7/2025	10.52
2102157	79.34	9/3/2024	
8523624	92.54	1/25/2025	
1230254	121.14	3/15/2024	
4236251	88.61	6/4/2025	
5320214	145.21	12/2/2025	
8236501	98.65	10/14/2024	
2362411	-25	9/15/2024	
5124715	226.25	11/25/2025	
8652147	-35.22	1/2/2024	
	1596.45		

Figure 3.15

Figure 3.16 shows the formula I created for my next example. Can you figure out what I am trying to accomplish before I explain it?

Chapter 3 – Functions, Formulas and Filters

=AVERAGE(D2:D18)/12	
D	E
Amount	
$112.25	
$36.32	
$118.25	
$152.22	
$77.26	
$83.21	
$115.37	
$89.41	
$73.25	
$126.21	
$75.33	
$99.21	
$175.85	
$186.54	
$128.58	
$56.21	
$8.88	

Figure 3.16

The goal here was to take the amount due for all the club members and then get the average total due. Then I took that total and divided it by 12 (for months of the year) to show the average amount due each month assuming they would pay their dues within a one year period.

As you can see, it's easy to create simple formulas in Excel to do basic calculations but once you start manipulating data within multiple rows, columns or even worksheets, things can get complicated quickly. For example, the text below shows an

Chapter 3 – Functions, Formulas and Filters

example of just how complex these Excel formulas can get. Can you figure out what the goal of this formula is? Neither can I!

=SUMPRODUCT(IFERROR(INDEX('Order Details'!$B$4:$B$1000, MATCH('Orders'!$A4,'Order Details'!$A$4:$A$1000,0),0),0),'Orders'!$D$4:$D$104)

Sorting Data

While adding data to your worksheet, you will most likely end up with multiple columns of information that might not be in the order you prefer. This is where sorting your data can really help you out.

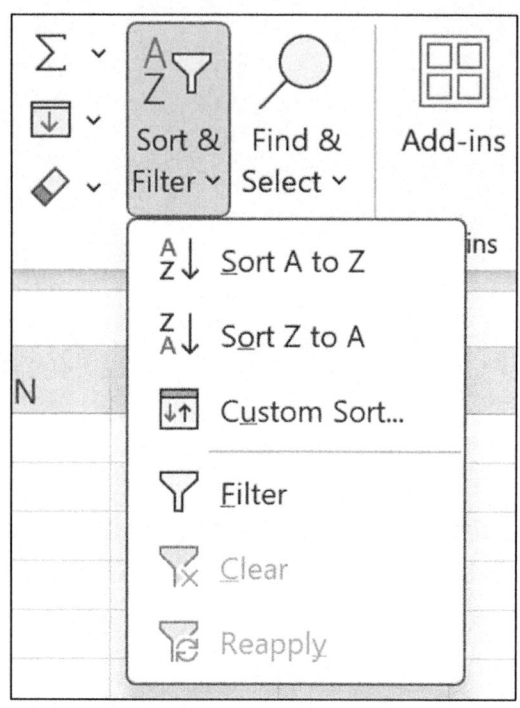

Figure 3.17

The most common type of sorting that you will do is to sort from smallest to largest or largest to smallest and that is why you have these two options at the top of the menu. If I were to select the same range of cells that I used in my filtering example, I would get a message similar to the one shown in Figure 3.18.

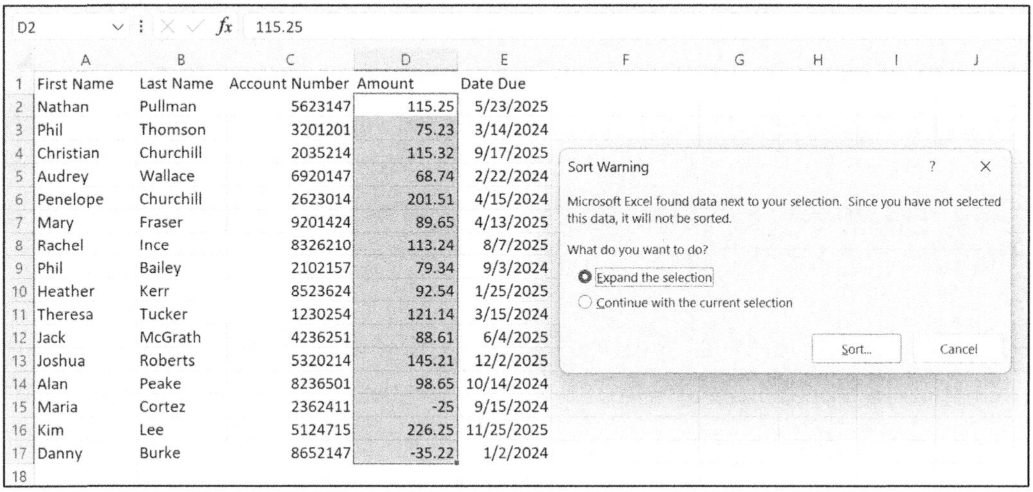

Chapter 3 – Functions, Formulas and Filters

Figure 3.18

When you sort data, you will most likely want to keep all the information in your rows together, so things do not get mixed up. If I were to sort the Amount column by lowest to highest and not sort the rest of the columns at the same time, the amount due would not match up with their name and account number etc.

If I choose the *Expand the selection* option, Excel will include the other columns in the sort procedure and then allow me to choose which column or columns to sort on (Figure 3.19).

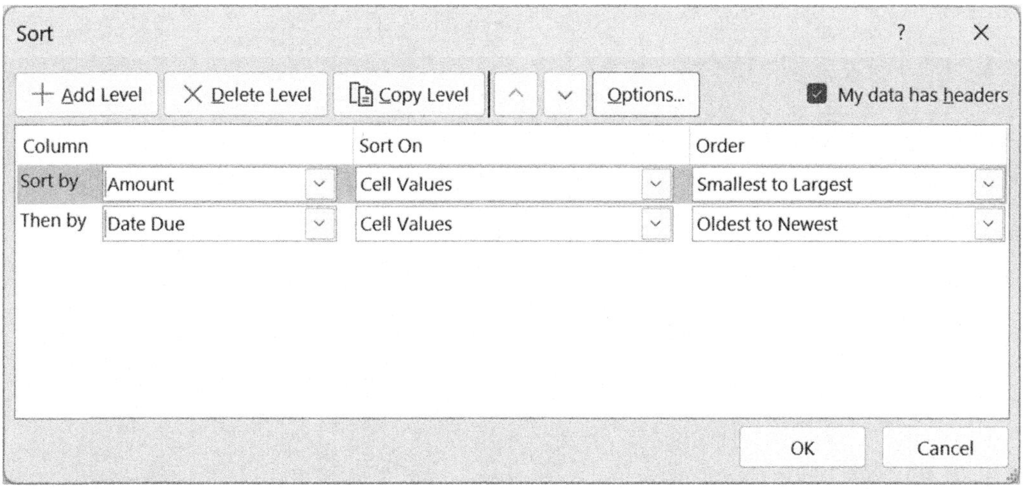

Figure 3.19

Now I can choose which columns I want to sort by. For this example, I will first sort by the amount due going from smallest to largest. Then I will have Excel do a secondary sort on the due date from oldest to newest. I will also make sure that the box labeled *My data has headers* is checked so Excel keeps the column titles at the top and doesn't sort them with the rest of the information.

If you look closely at Figure 3.20, you will see that the Amount column is sorted by smallest to largest, but the Due Date column is not sorted by oldest to newest. This is because the Amount column was the primary sort option and the dates have to stay with the amount, so they just happen to end up where they end up. So keep that in mind when sorting your data on more than one column.

Chapter 3 – Functions, Formulas and Filters

	A	B	C	D	E
1	First Name	Last Name	Account Number	Amount	Date Due
2	Danny	Burke	8652147	-35.22	1/2/2024
3	Maria	Cortez	2362411	-25	9/15/2024
4	Audrey	Wallace	6920147	68.74	2/22/2024
5	Phil	Thomson	3201201	75.23	3/14/2024
6	Phil	Bailey	2102157	79.34	9/3/2024
7	Jack	McGrath	4236251	88.61	6/4/2025
8	Mary	Fraser	9201424	89.65	4/13/2025
9	Heather	Kerr	8523624	92.54	1/25/2025
10	Alan	Peake	8236501	98.65	10/14/2024
11	Rachel	Ince	8326210	113.24	8/7/2025
12	Nathan	Pullman	5623147	115.25	5/23/2025
13	Christian	Churchill	2035214	115.32	9/17/2025
14	Theresa	Tucker	1230254	121.14	3/15/2024
15	Joshua	Roberts	5320214	145.21	12/2/2025
16	Penelope	Churchill	2623014	201.51	4/15/2024
17	Kim	Lee	5124715	226.25	11/25/2025
18					

Figure 3.20

Figure 3.21 shows a different worksheet that has some other columns that will work with a multi-level sort.

	A	B	C	D	E	F	G	H
1	First Name	Last Name	Account Number	Amount	Date Due	Package Letter	Service Level	Advisor Name
2	John	Hodges	1265425	$112.25	2/25/2023	A	1	Joe
3	Neil	Fisher	3625147	$36.32	3/14/2024	A	2	Jessie
4	Julian	Bell	3623621	$118.25	9/14/2024	C	1	Maria
5	Brandon	Harris	6358474	$152.22	1/25/2025	B	4	Maria
6	Grace	Lyman	2514255	$77.26	5/30/2024	C	2	Joe
7	Emily	Metcalfe	5542789	$83.21	12/14/2023	B	3	Tom
8	Sebastian	Taylor	3262517	$115.37	8/22/2024	A	3	Joe
9	Andrea	King	5652147	$89.41	9/15/2025	C	2	Maria
10	Samantha	Alsop	7562551	$73.25	11/3/2024	C	4	Tom
11	Leonard	Smith	5532149	$126.21	7/21/2024	B	4	Jessie
12	Megan	Lewis	2235448	$75.33	10/15/2024	A	1	Joe
13	Austin	Mackenzie	4426821	$99.21	2/22/2025	C	2	Tom
14	Sonia	Ince	9865277	$175.85	6/14/2025	B	4	Maria
15	Anthony	Glover	3265147	$186.54	5/15/2025	B	2	Jessie
16	Sally	Terry	8952147	$128.58	5/18/2025	A	3	Tom
17	Joe	Hart	3352776	$56.21	12/22/2024	C	1	Joe
18								

Figure 3.28

Chapter 3 – Functions, Formulas and Filters

I will sort the data on *Package Letter* first and then *Advisor name* second. Figure 3.22 shows that the Package Letter column is sorted from A to C. Then you can see that the Advisor Name column is sorted by name but corresponds separately to each Package Letter.

	A	B	C	D	E	F	G	H
1	First Name	Last Name	Account Number	Amount	Date Due	Package Letter	Service Level	Advisor Name
2	Neil	Fisher	3625147	$36.32	3/14/2024	A	2	Jessie
3	John	Hodges	1265425	$112.25	2/25/2023	A	1	Joe
4	Sebastian	Taylor	3262517	$115.37	8/22/2024	A	3	Joe
5	Megan	Lewis	2235448	$75.33	10/15/2024	A	1	Joe
6	Sally	Terry	8952147	$128.58	5/18/2025	A	3	Tom
7	Leonard	Smith	5532149	$126.21	7/21/2024	B	4	Jessie
8	Anthony	Glover	3265147	$186.54	5/15/2025	B	2	Jessie
9	Brandon	Harris	6358474	$152.22	1/25/2025	B	4	Maria
10	Sonia	Ince	9865277	$175.85	6/14/2025	B	4	Maria
11	Emily	Metcalfe	5542789	$83.21	12/14/2023	B	3	Tom
12	Grace	Lyman	2514255	$77.26	5/30/2024	C	2	Joe
13	Joe	Hart	3352776	$56.21	12/22/2024	C	1	Joe
14	Julian	Bell	3623621	$118.25	9/14/2024	C	1	Maria
15	Andrea	King	5652147	$89.41	9/15/2025	C	2	Maria
16	Samantha	Alsop	7562551	$73.25	11/3/2024	C	4	Tom
17	Austin	Mackenzie	4426821	$99.21	2/22/2025	C	2	Tom
18								

Figure 3.22

Chapter 4 – Formatting Your Workbook

Now that we have some data on our worksheets, it's time to make it look more appealing and at the same time, get it ready for printing. Sure, you can format your worksheets as you go along so that is completely up to you. If you do end up formatting as you go along, you might find yourself having to reformat something because you changed your style after the fact though.

Adding Cell Borders
One of the easiest things you can to do make your data easier to read and appear more organized is to add borders to your cells. Even though it looks like the cells already have borders, those grey boxes are actually gridlines and will not show up when you print or export your worksheet.

To apply a border to a cell or group of cells, you will need to select (highlight) them first and then you can choose a border style from the *Home* tab in the *Fonts* group. Figure 4.1 shows the borders dropdown selection menu and as you can see, there are several border types to choose from.

Chapter 4 – Formatting Your Workbook

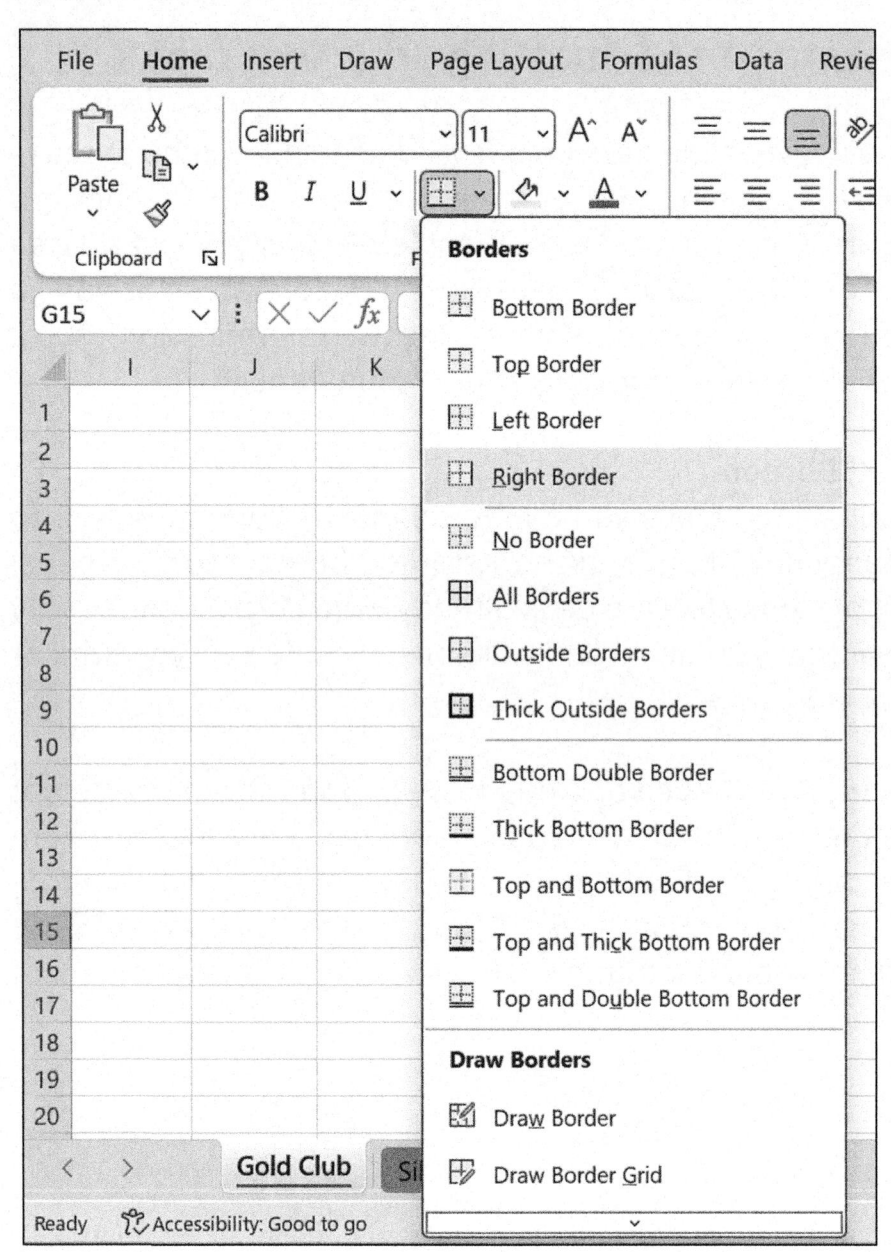

Figure 4.1

If you were to click the arrow icon at the lower right corner of the Fonts group, you would then be shown additional options when you click on the *Border* tab. Here you can change the style and color of the border as well as add diagonal lines as seen in Figure 4.3.

Chapter 4 – Formatting Your Workbook

Figure 4.2

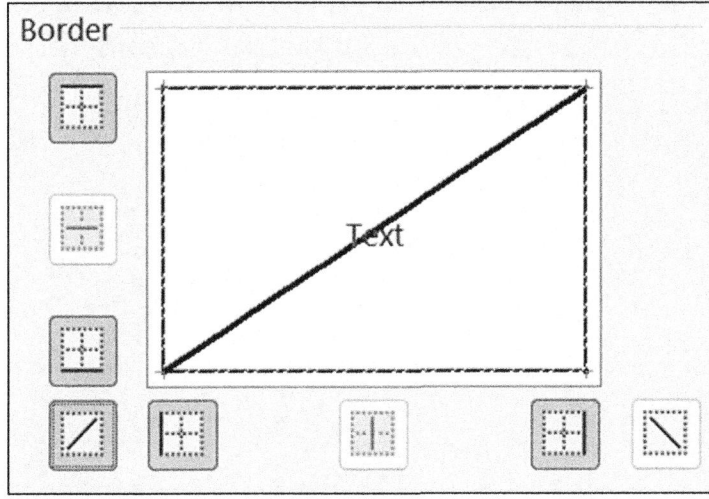

Figure 4.3

Chapter 4 – Formatting Your Workbook

I will now select all the cells that have my data in one of my worksheets and then apply the *All Borders* style border to the cells as seen in Figure 4.4.

	A	B	C	D	E
1	First Name	Last Name	Account Num	Amount	Date Due
2	Vanessa	Watson	5232148	$121.52	1/23/2025
3	Dylan	Bond	4251575	$83.25	7/5/2024
4	Nathan	Morgan	6562541	$53.87	8/17/2024
5	Christian	Clarkson	4523217	$75.25	5/15/2024
6	Victoria	Dyer	4515482	$101.00	9/22/2025
7	Phil	Randall	3625145	$112.25	10/15/2024
8	Claire	Ogden	3265147	$86.21	12/3/2024
9	Jan	Clark	9562147	$97.24	8/27/2025
10	Connor	Mathis	3265147	$118.32	8/6/2025
11	Jessica	McGrath	2233517	$198.98	9/17/2025
12	Brian	Randall	9532214	$58.21	11/5/2024
13	Natalie	Baker	9215714	$136.84	1/26/2024
14	Cameron	Welch	3215412	$147.98	11/15/2024
15	Anthony	Lewis	8762514	$26.25	5/4/2025
16	Luke	Simpson	5621514	$89.27	3/2/2024
17	Amy	Avery	7563214	$139.75	2/19/2025
18	Neil	Graham	2124214	$205.63	12/15/2024
19					
20	Total			$1,646.19	

Figure 4.4

I will then apply the *Thick Bottom Border* style to row 1 and then the *Thick Outside Borders* style to cell D20 which has my amount total.

Chapter 4 – Formatting Your Workbook

	A	B	C	D	E
1	First Name	Last Name	Account Num	Amount	Date Due
2	Vanessa	Watson	5232148	$121.52	1/23/2025
3	Dylan	Bond	4251575	$83.25	7/5/2024
4	Nathan	Morgan	6562541	$53.87	8/17/2024
5	Christian	Clarkson	4523217	$75.25	5/15/2024
6	Victoria	Dyer	4515482	$101.00	9/22/2025
7	Phil	Randall	3625145	$112.25	10/15/2024
8	Claire	Ogden	3265147	$86.21	12/3/2024
9	Jan	Clark	9562147	$97.24	8/27/2025
10	Connor	Mathis	3265147	$118.32	8/6/2025
11	Jessica	McGrath	2233517	$198.98	9/17/2025
12	Brian	Randall	9532214	$58.21	11/5/2024
13	Natalie	Baker	9215714	$136.84	1/26/2024
14	Cameron	Welch	3215412	$147.98	11/15/2024
15	Anthony	Lewis	8762514	$26.25	5/4/2025
16	Luke	Simpson	5621514	$89.27	3/2/2024
17	Amy	Avery	7563214	$139.75	2/19/2025
18	Neil	Graham	2124214	$205.63	12/15/2024
19					
20	Total			$1,646.19	

Figure 4.5

One thing to keep in mind is that if you apply one type of border to a range of cells and then apply a different type of border to part of that range, you might find that the new border style has overwritten some of the cell edges that you didn't intend for it to do. When this happens, you can simply reapply that style to the cells that have been affected.

Adding Colors to Cells
Another way to make your spreadsheet stand out and easier to work with is to add colors to your cells. This can be done to do things such as color code specific categories or make your column headers stand out etc.

To apply colors to your cells, simply select the cells you wish to add the color to and then from the Home tab and the Font group, select

Chapter 4 – Formatting Your Workbook

the cell fill color icon and choose a color from the available choices.

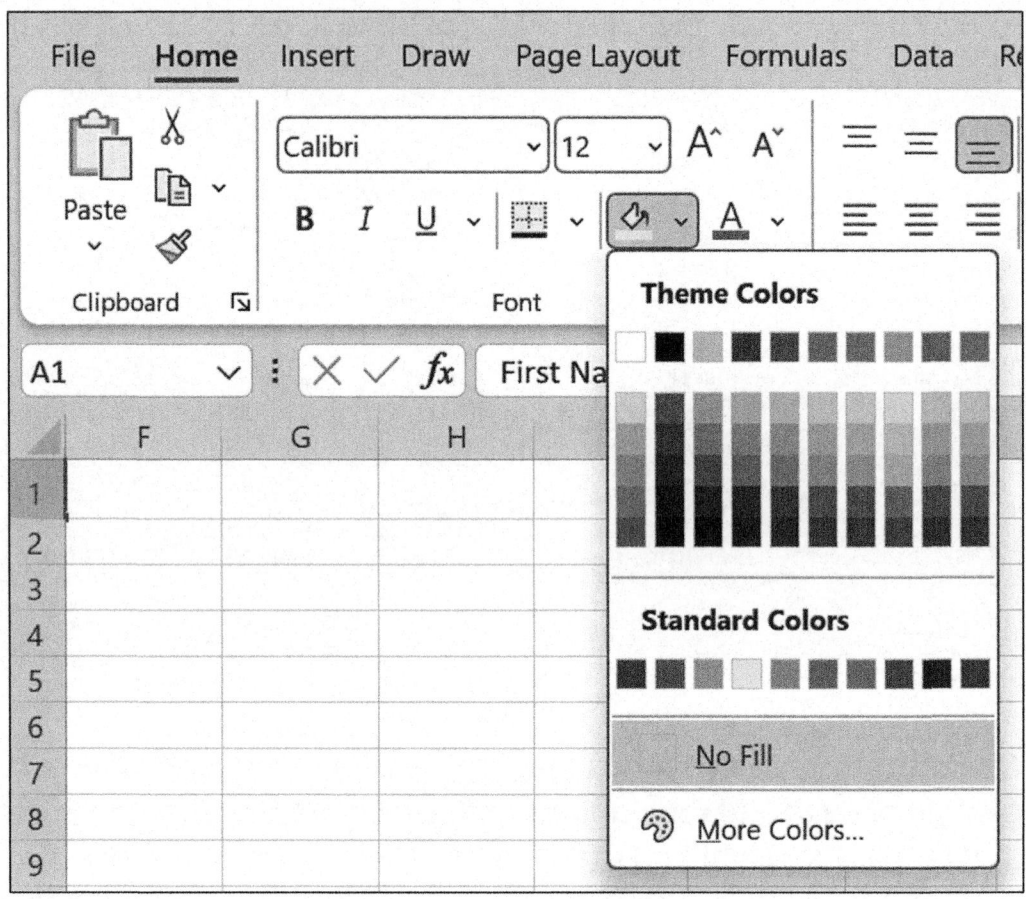

Figure 4.6

If you do not like any of the theme or standard colors, you can click on *More Colors* to see additional choices or to create your own custom color. If you apply a color to a cell and want to remove it, you can come back here and choose the *No Fill* option. Don't choose the white color because that is not the same as removing the color itself.

I will now fill the cells with my column headers with one color and then the cell with my amount total with a different color.

Chapter 4 – Formatting Your Workbook

	A	B	C	D	E
1	First Name	Last Name	Account Num	Amount	Date Due
2	Vanessa	Watson	5232148	$121.52	1/23/2025
3	Dylan	Bond	4251575	$83.25	7/5/2024
4	Nathan	Morgan	6562541	$53.87	8/17/2024
5	Christian	Clarkson	4523217	$75.25	5/15/2024
6	Victoria	Dyer	4515482	$101.00	9/22/2025
7	Phil	Randall	3625145	$112.25	10/15/2024
8	Claire	Ogden	3265147	$86.21	12/3/2024
9	Jan	Clark	9562147	$97.24	8/27/2025
10	Connor	Mathis	3265147	$118.32	8/6/2025
11	Jessica	McGrath	2233517	$198.98	9/17/2025
12	Brian	Randall	9532214	$58.21	11/5/2024
13	Natalie	Baker	9215714	$136.84	1/26/2024
14	Cameron	Welch	3215412	$147.98	11/15/2024
15	Anthony	Lewis	8762514	$26.25	5/4/2025
16	Luke	Simpson	5621514	$89.27	3/2/2024
17	Amy	Avery	7563214	$139.75	2/19/2025
18	Neil	Graham	2124214	$205.63	12/15/2024
19					
20	Total			$1,646.19	

Figure 4.7

When using cell colors, be sure not to overdo it because you will find that it makes things harder to see compared to not having any colors at all.

Changing Font Attributes

If you have ever changed font settings in other programs such as Microsoft Word for example, then you will have no problem changing font settings in Excel. Many people find that the default font attributes work just fine but if you are the type who likes to make their work stand out a bit, then you can change these attributes as needed.

To change font settings, simply select the cell or cells you wish to adjust and then go to the *Font* group on the *Home* tab. Here you will see the typical font settings such as bold, italics and

Chapter 4 – Formatting Your Workbook

underlined. You can also change the size and color of the font as needed. And if you want to change the font itself, you can select a new one from the font drop down menu.

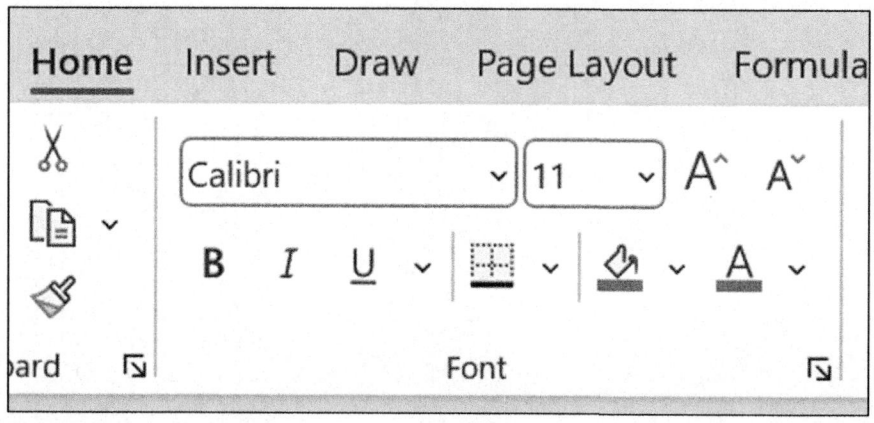

Figure 4.8

If you click the arrow at the lower right corner of the Font group, you will see have some additional ways to change your type settings when you click on the *Font* tab.

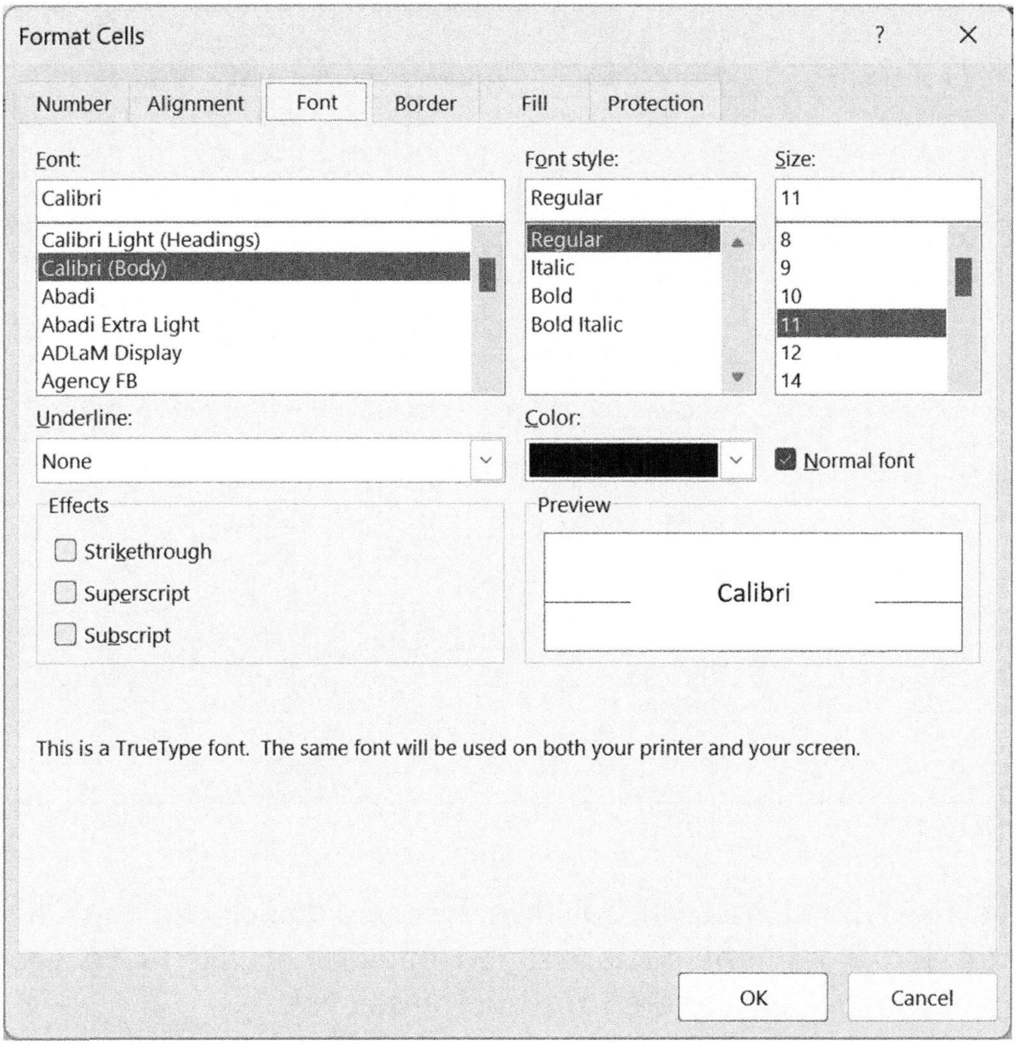

Chapter 4 – Formatting Your Workbook

Figure 4.9

I will now make my column heading font bold as well as change it to a different font altogether to make it stand out. I will also make my amount total bold and add a double underline to it as well.

Chapter 4 – Formatting Your Workbook

	A	B	C	D	E
1	**First Name**	**Last Name**	**Account Nur**	**Amount**	**Date Due**
2	Vanessa	Watson	5232148	$121.52	1/23/2025
3	Dylan	Bond	4251575	$83.25	7/5/2024
4	Nathan	Morgan	6562541	$53.87	8/17/2024
5	Christian	Clarkson	4523217	$75.25	5/15/2024
6	Victoria	Dyer	4515482	$101.00	9/22/2025
7	Phil	Randall	3625145	$112.25	10/15/2024
8	Claire	Ogden	3265147	$86.21	12/3/2024
9	Jan	Clark	9562147	$97.24	8/27/2025
10	Connor	Mathis	3265147	$118.32	8/6/2025
11	Jessica	McGrath	2233517	$198.98	9/17/2025
12	Brian	Randall	9532214	$58.21	11/5/2024
13	Natalie	Baker	9215714	$136.84	1/26/2024
14	Cameron	Welch	3215412	$147.98	11/15/2024
15	Anthony	Lewis	8762514	$26.25	5/4/2025
16	Luke	Simpson	5621514	$89.27	3/2/2024
17	Amy	Avery	7563214	$139.75	2/19/2025
18	Neil	Graham	2124214	$205.63	12/15/2024
19					
20	Total			$1,646.19	

Figure 4.10

Just like I mentioned with cell fill colors, you do not want to go too wild with your font customization because it will make your spreadsheet look cluttered and unprofessional.

Adjusting Cell Width and Height

As you type data into your cells, you have most likely noticed that you only have a certain amount of space within a cell to fit your information. Then when you go over the width of the cell, the data appears to start filling the next cell over. Even though it appears this way, this is not the case and it's very easy to adjust the row height or column width to make your data fit properly.

Chapter 4 – Formatting Your Workbook

Text Alignment

You might have noticed that Excel decides for itself how your data will be aligned within your cells. Generally, numbers and dates are aligned to the right while text is aligned to the left. If you do not like the way your data is aligned within your cells, you can easily change it.

Figure 4.11 shows a worksheet where column B is too wide and column C is too narrow and even column D can use a little adjustment.

	A	B	C	D	E
1	First Name	Last Name	Account Nur	Amount	Date Due
2	John	Hodges	1265425	$112.25	2/25/2023
3	Neil	Fisher	3625147	$36.32	3/14/2024
4	Julian	Bell	3623621	$118.25	9/14/2024
5	Brandon	Harris	6358474	$152.22	1/25/2025
6	Grace	Lyman	2514255	$77.26	5/30/2024
7	Emily	Metcalfe	5542789	$83.21	12/14/2023
8	Sebastian	Taylor	3262517	$115.37	8/22/2024
9	Andrea	King	5652147	$89.41	9/15/2025
10	Samantha	Alsop	7562551	$73.25	11/3/2024
11	Leonard	Smith	5532149	$126.21	7/21/2024
12	Megan	Lewis	2235448	$75.33	10/15/2024
13	Austin	Mackenzie	4426821	$99.21	2/22/2025
14	Sonia	Ince	9865277	$175.85	6/14/2025
15	Anthony	Glover	3265147	$186.54	5/15/2025
16	Sally	Terry	8952147	$128.58	5/18/2025
17	Joe	Hart	3352776	$56.21	12/22/2024
18					

Figure 4.11

To manually change the width of column B, I will place my mouse cursor between the cells B and C but over the grey area where the column letters are until I see a double sided arrow. Then I can simply drag with my mouse and adjust the width of the column as needed. This also applies to rows.

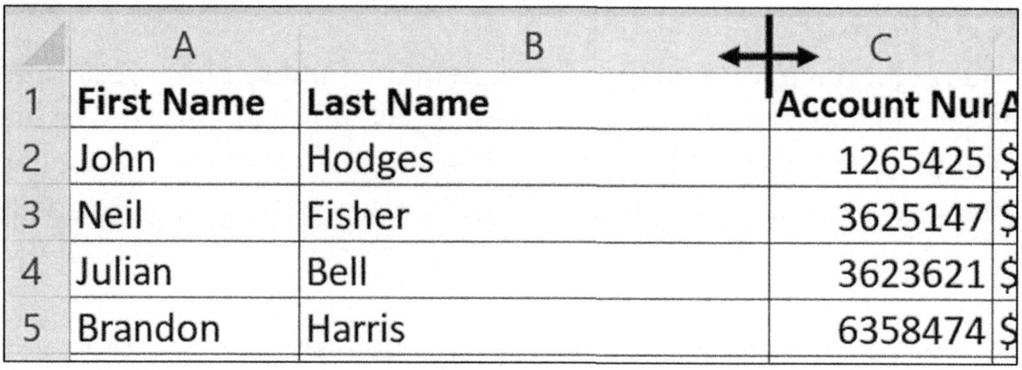

Chapter 4 – Formatting Your Workbook

	A	B	C
1	**First Name**	**Last Name**	**Account Nur**
2	John	Hodges	1265425
3	Neil	Fisher	3625147
4	Julian	Bell	3623621
5	Brandon	Harris	6358474

Figure 4.12

If you want to resize all your columns at once and have them all be sized to fit the data within that column, you can click on the top left corner to the left of A and above 1 to highlight the entire worksheet.

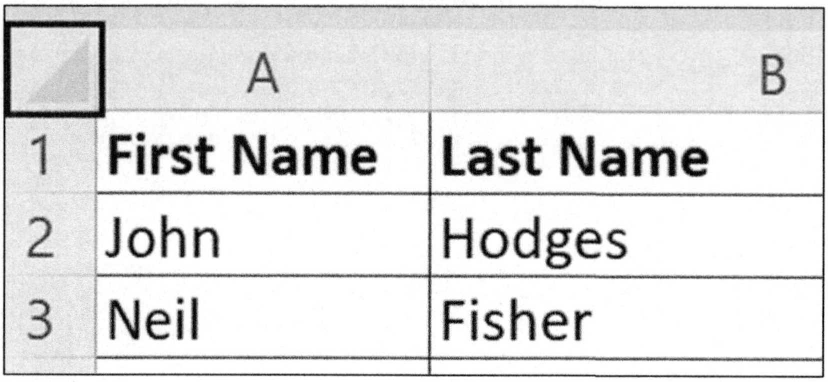

	A	B
1	**First Name**	**Last Name**
2	John	Hodges
3	Neil	Fisher

Figure 4.13

Once the entire worksheet has been selected, you can place your cursor between two cells like you did before to make the double sided arrow and then double click to have everything adjusted to fit as seen in Figure 4.14.

Chapter 4 – Formatting Your Workbook

	A	B	C	D	E
1	First Name	Last Name	Account Number	Amount	Date Due
2	John	Hodges	1265425	$112.25	2/25/2023
3	Neil	Fisher	3625147	$36.32	3/14/2024
4	Julian	Bell	3623621	$118.25	9/14/2024
5	Brandon	Harris	6358474	$152.22	1/25/2025
6	Grace	Lyman	2514255	$77.26	5/30/2024
7	Emily	Metcalfe	5542789	$83.21	12/14/2023
8	Sebastian	Taylor	3262517	$115.37	8/22/2024
9	Andrea	King	5652147	$89.41	9/15/2025
10	Samantha	Alsop	7562551	$73.25	11/3/2024
11	Leonard	Smith	5532149	$126.21	7/21/2024
12	Megan	Lewis	2235448	$75.33	10/15/2024
13	Austin	Mackenzie	4426821	$99.21	2/22/2025
14	Sonia	Ince	9865277	$175.85	6/14/2025
15	Anthony	Glover	3265147	$186.54	5/15/2025
16	Sally	Terry	8952147	$128.58	5/18/2025
17	Joe	Hart	3352776	$56.21	12/22/2024

Figure 4.14

As you can see, Excel made the column width fit the longest item in that column. So for column C, it's bigger than the rest because the *Account Number* header is on the longer side.

Now let's say I want to adjust the height of my rows so things don't look so cluttered. I will enlarge the size of row 4 with my mouse to find the look I am going for. Then rather and try to eyeball the rest of my rows to make the match, I can right click row 4 and select *Row height* to see that the size is 22.8 as shown in figure 4.15.

Chapter 4 – Formatting Your Workbook

	A	B	C	D	E
1	First Name	Last Name	Account Number	Amount	Date Due
2	John	Hodges	1265425	$112.25	2/25/2023
3	Neil	Fisher	3625147	$36.32	3/14/2024
4	Julian	Bell	3623621	$118.25	9/14/2024
5	Brandon	Harris		2	1/25/2025
6	Grace	Lyman			5/30/2024
7	Emily	Metcalfe			12/14/2023
8	Sebastian	Taylor		7	8/22/2024
9	Andrea	King			9/15/2025
10	Samantha	Alsop	7562551	$73.25	11/3/2024
11	Leonard	Smith	5532149	$126.21	7/21/2024

Row Height dialog: Row height: 22.8

Figure 4.15

Now I can manually type in 22.8 for each row or I can select all the rows I want to adjust, right click on any of them, choose Row height and type in 22.8 just once to have it applied to all of them as shown in figure 4.16.

	A	B	C	D	E
1	First Name	Last Name	Account Number	Amount	Date Due
2	John	Hodges	1265425	$112.25	2/25/2023
3	Neil	Fisher	3625147	$36.32	3/14/2024
4	Julian	Bell	3623621	$118.25	9/14/2024
5	Brandon	Harris	6358474	$152.22	1/25/2025
6	Grace	Lyman	2514255	$77.26	5/30/2024
7	Emily	Metcalfe	5542789	$83.21	12/14/2023
8	Sebastian	Taylor	3262517	$115.37	8/22/2024

Figure 4.16

Chapter 4 – Formatting Your Workbook

Now I would like to take a moment to mention the Word Wrap feature of Excel. This comes in handy when you have a lot of data in a cell but do not want to stretch it out and make the row longer than you would like it to be.

Figure 4.17 shows an auto repair list, and the Diagnostic column contains data that is too long to fit within the cell. I can expand column C to make everything fit but that might make it run off the page when I go to print it.

	A	B	C	D
1	Name	Model	Diagnostic	Estimate
2	Maria Torres	Mustang	Needs all new belts and a	$299.00
3	Mary King	F-150	Full service and tire rotatio	$150.00
4	Rachel Foster	Impreza	Replace the rear shocks ar	$429.00
5	Heather Smith	Accord	Change spark plugs.	$199.00
6	Kim Daniels	Camry	New tires and front brake	$775.00
7	Jack Baker	Tacoma	Transmission service	$199.00

Figure 4.17

What I can do instead is format the cell using *Word Wrap* which will force the data to fit in the cell and be viewable. Then if you were to change the size of the cell to make it taller or wider, the data within that cell would change to fit as well. To apply this text wrapping to my cells I will select them, right click any of the cells and choose *Format Cells*. Then in the alignment tab, I will check the box that says *Wrap text*.

Chapter 4 – Formatting Your Workbook

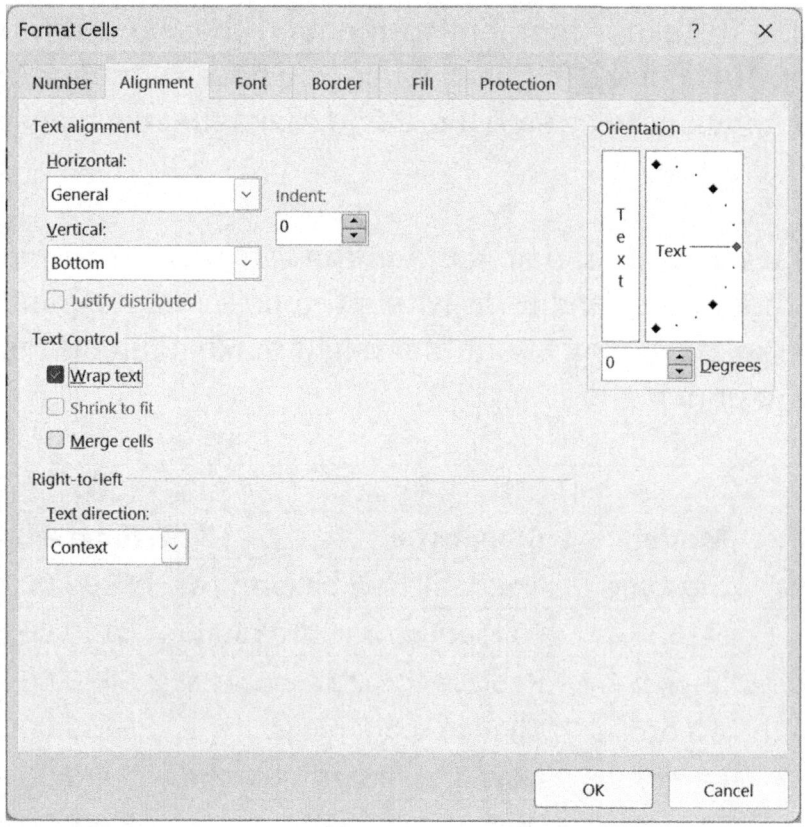

Figure 4.18

Now the text in column C fits in the cell and if I were to resize the row or column size, the text would automatically adjust itself to fit.

	A	B	C	D
1	Name	Model	Diagnostic	Estimate
2	Maria Torres	Mustang	Needs all new belts and a radiator flush.	$299.00
3	Mary King	F-150	Full service and tire rotation.	$150.00
4	Rachel Foster	Impreza	Replace the rear shocks and do an all wheel alignment.	$429.00
5	Heather Smith	Accord	Change spark plugs.	$199.00
6	Kim Daniels	Camry	New tires and front brake pads.	$775.00
7	Jack Baker	Tacoma	Transmission service	$199.00
8				

Figure 4.19

Using Styles and Conditional Formatting

If you are the type that is not satisfied with simply changing the colors of your cells or would like to apply formatting to your cells that reflects the data within those cells, then applying styles and conditional formatting might be the answer for you.

You can think of styles kind of like themes where you have custom attributes for things such as cell colors, font size and type, and cell formatting for things such as currency or percentages.

To apply a style to your worksheet, simply highlight the data you want it to apply to and then click on *Cell Styles* from the *Home* tab.

As you can see in Figure 4.20, there are several style attributes to choose from such as cell and text color, header size, accent colors and number formats. You can hover your mouse over each type and see how it will look if it were to be applied to your worksheet.

Chapter 4 – Formatting Your Workbook

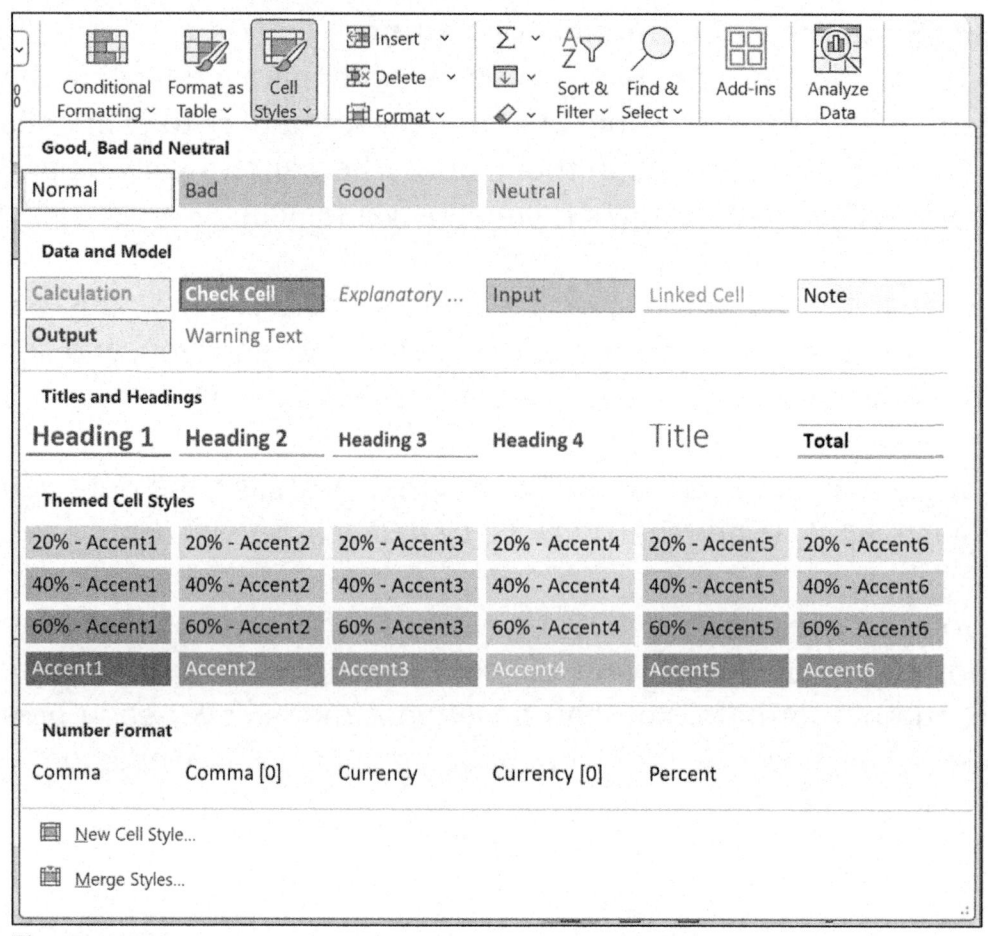

Figure 4.20

If you were to click on *New Cell Style,* you would then be able to create your own style that you can use as needed.

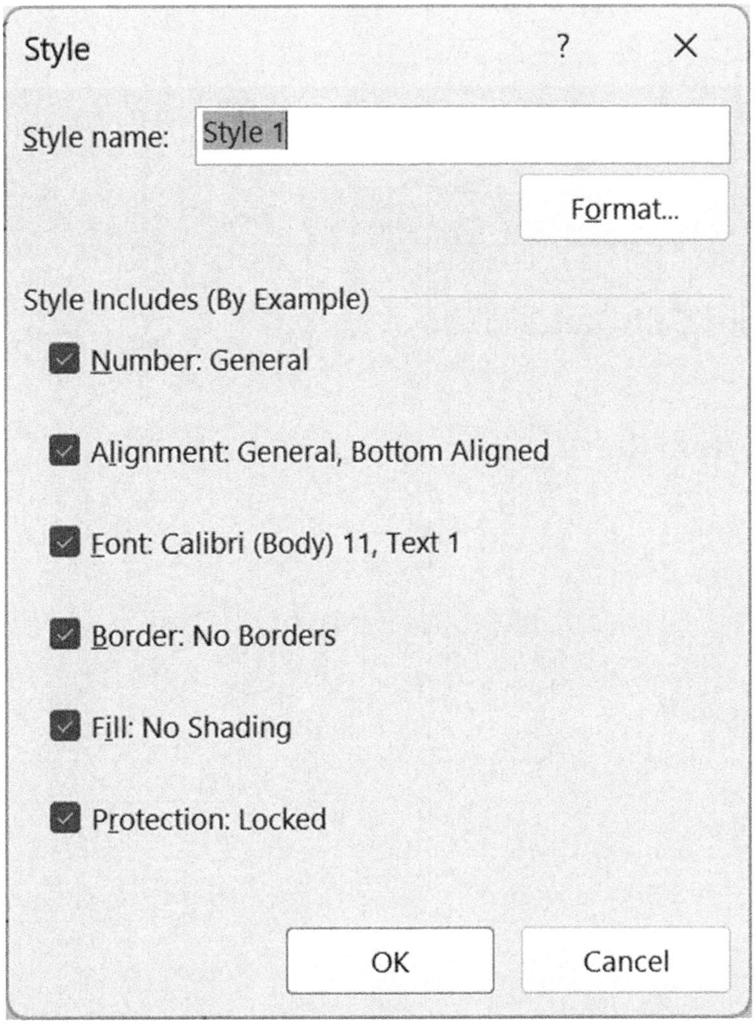

Chapter 4 – Formatting Your Workbook

Figure 4.21

Conditional formatting is a little more involved and it allows you to format your cells based on their contents. When you click on the Conditional Formatting button from the Home tab, you will see that there are various types of formatting that you can apply to your data.

Chapter 4 – Formatting Your Workbook

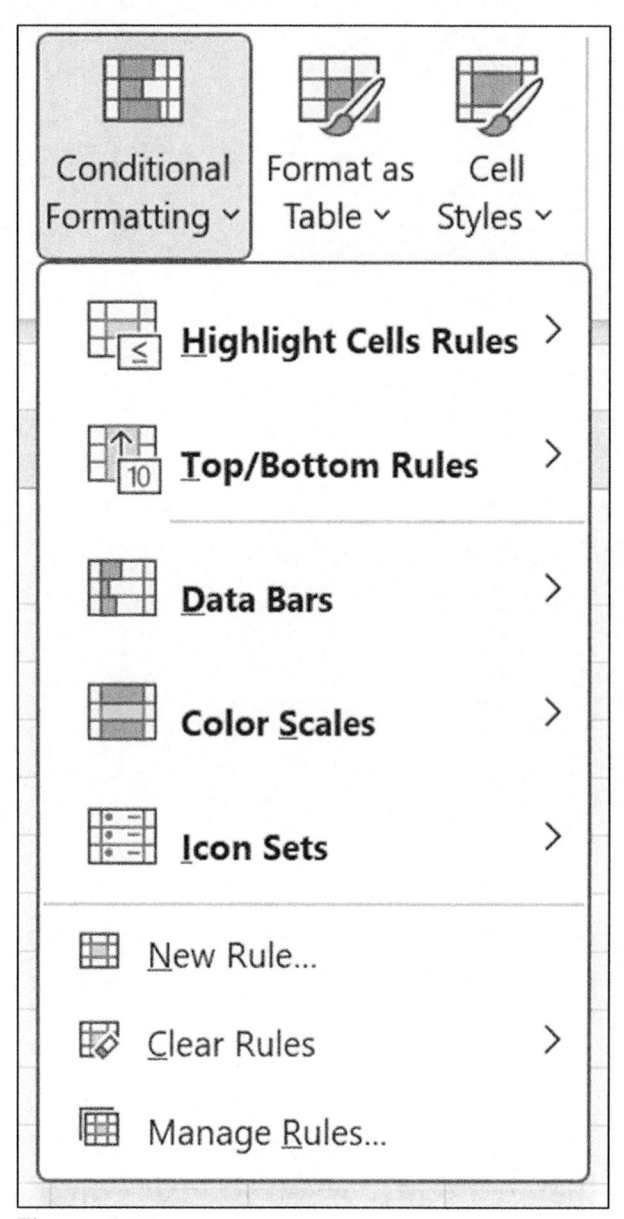

Figure 4.22

For example, if I were to highlight the data in my amount column and then apply the *Highlight Cells Rules* and choose the *Between* option (Figure 4.23), I would then need to enter in the numbers I want this rule to apply to (Figure 4.24).

Chapter 4 – Formatting Your Workbook

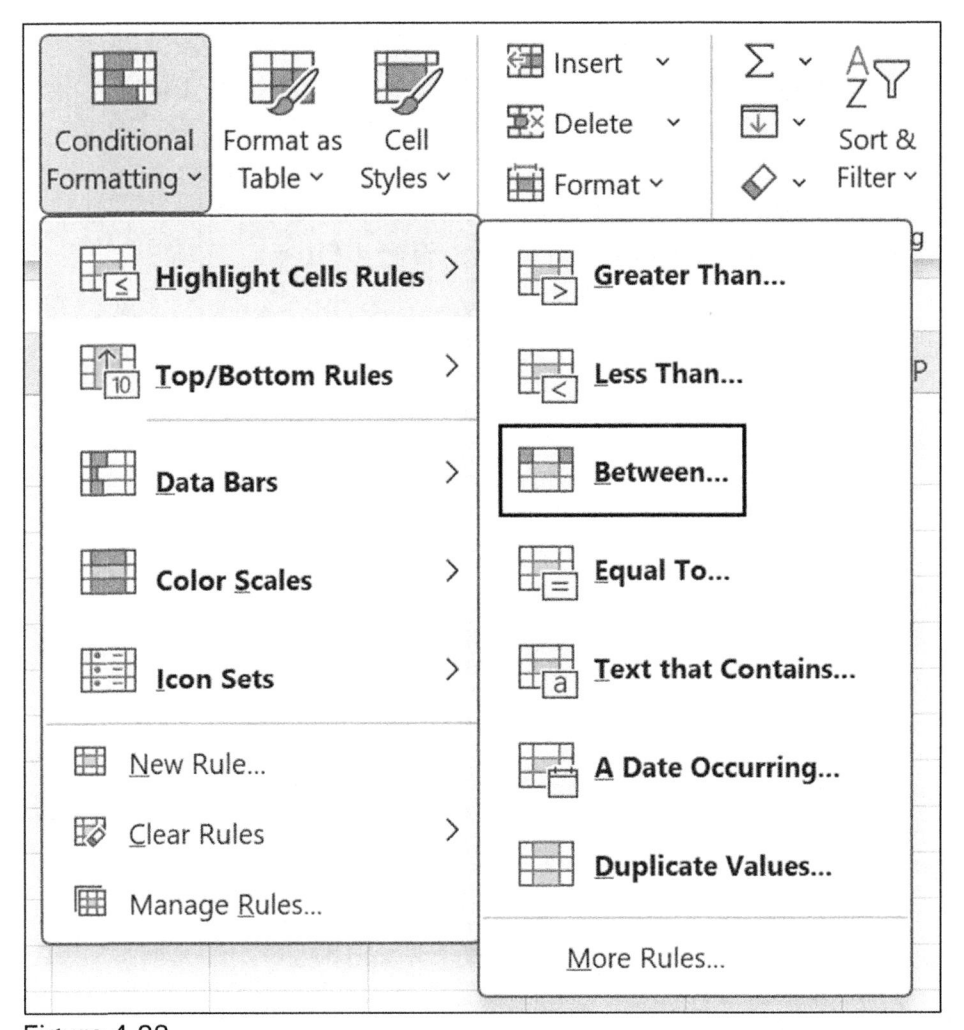

Figure 4.23

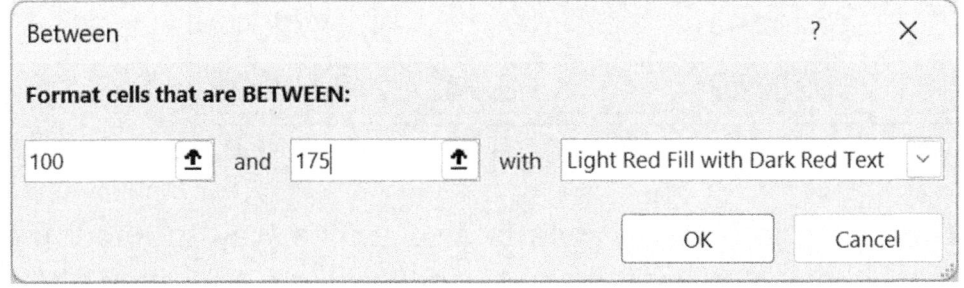

Figure 4.24

Since I have entered 100 and 175, this means Excel will highlight any cells that contain numbers between these two values with a light red fill with dark red text. I can change the color scheme by

Chapter 4 – Formatting Your Workbook

clicking the down arrow next to it if needed. Figure 4.25 shows the results of the conditional formatting that has been applied.

C	D	E
Account Number	**Amount**	**Date Due**
2102157	79.34	9/3/2024
8652147	-35.22	1/2/2024
2623014	201.51	4/15/2024
2035214	115.32	9/17/2025
2362411	-25	9/15/2024
9201424	89.65	4/13/2025
8326210	113.24	8/7/2025
8523624	92.54	1/25/2025
5124715	226.25	11/25/2025
4236251	88.61	6/4/2025
8236501	98.65	10/14/2024
5623147	115.25	5/23/2025
5320214	145.21	12/2/2025
3201201	75.23	3/14/2024
1230254	121.14	3/15/2024
6920147	68.74	2/22/2024

Figure 4.25

The *Data Bars* formatting style is also a nice way to show the relationship between the data in your cells. Figure 4.26 shows how my amount column looks after applying a gradient fill to it. As you can see, the larger numbers have a larger bar going across the cell while the negative numbers have bars going in the opposite direction and are a different color.

Chapter 4 – Formatting Your Workbook

C	D	E
Account Number	**Amount**	**Date Due**
2102157	79.34	9/3/2024
8652147	-35.22	1/2/2024
2623014	201.51	4/15/2024
2035214	115.32	9/17/2025
2362411	-25	9/15/2024
9201424	89.65	4/13/2025
8326210	113.24	8/7/2025
8523624	92.54	1/25/2025
5124715	226.25	11/25/2025
4236251	88.61	6/4/2025
8236501	98.65	10/14/2024
5623147	115.25	5/23/2025
5320214	145.21	12/2/2025
3201201	75.23	3/14/2024
1230254	121.14	3/15/2024
6920147	68.74	2/22/2024

Figure 4.26

Rules are used to create your own custom conditional formatting and allow you to fine tune how the formatting is applied to your cells. As you can see from Figure 4.27, there are many settings you can configure when creating a new rule.

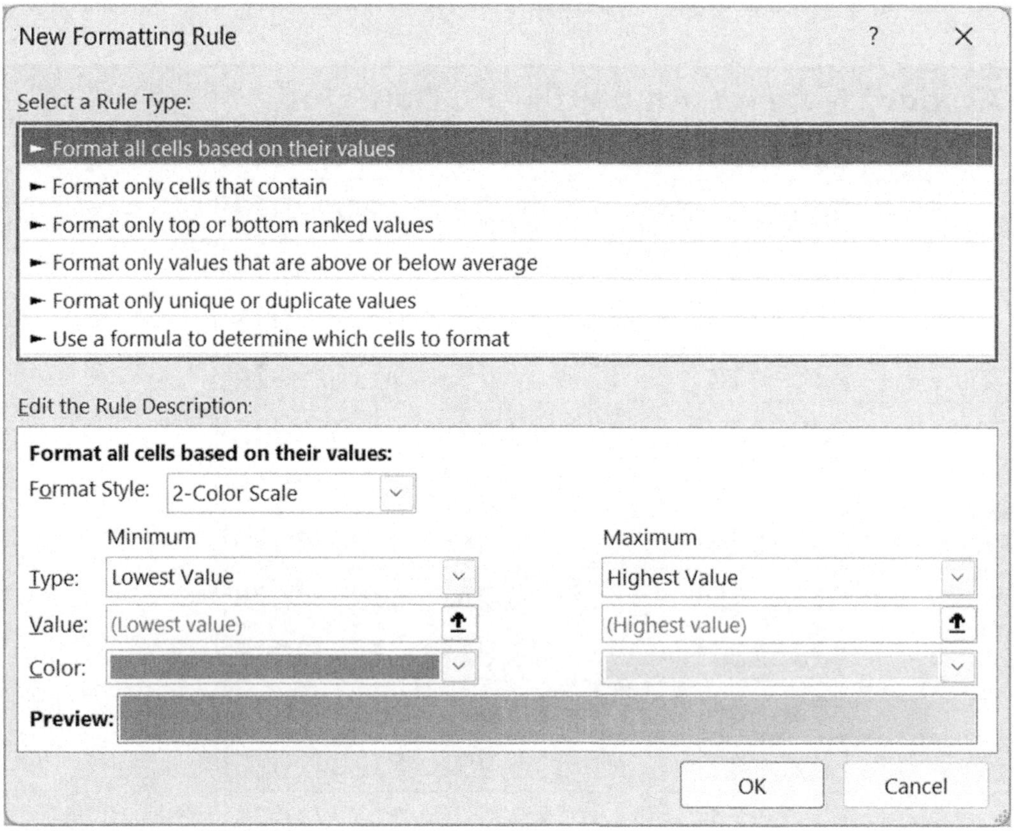

Chapter 4 – Formatting Your Workbook

Figure 4.27

Formatting Cells for Numbers

Since working with numbers is such a huge part of using Microsoft Excel, it makes sense that there would be multiple ways to format your cells based on what type of numeric data you have in these cells.

If you simply type in a number by itself, Excel will format it using the General setting which pretty much means no formatting at all. If you were to type in a number with a $ sign in front of it such as $25, Excel would automatically apply the Currency format to that cell.

Just because you type in a number a certain way, doesn't mean you are stuck with that cell format type. You can easily apply different

Chapter 4 – Formatting Your Workbook

formatting to your cells as needed or simply add your numbers and format them later.

If you were to right click a cell with a number or even no data at all, you would then be able to choose the *Format Cells* choice and be shown the available options as seen in Figure 4.28.

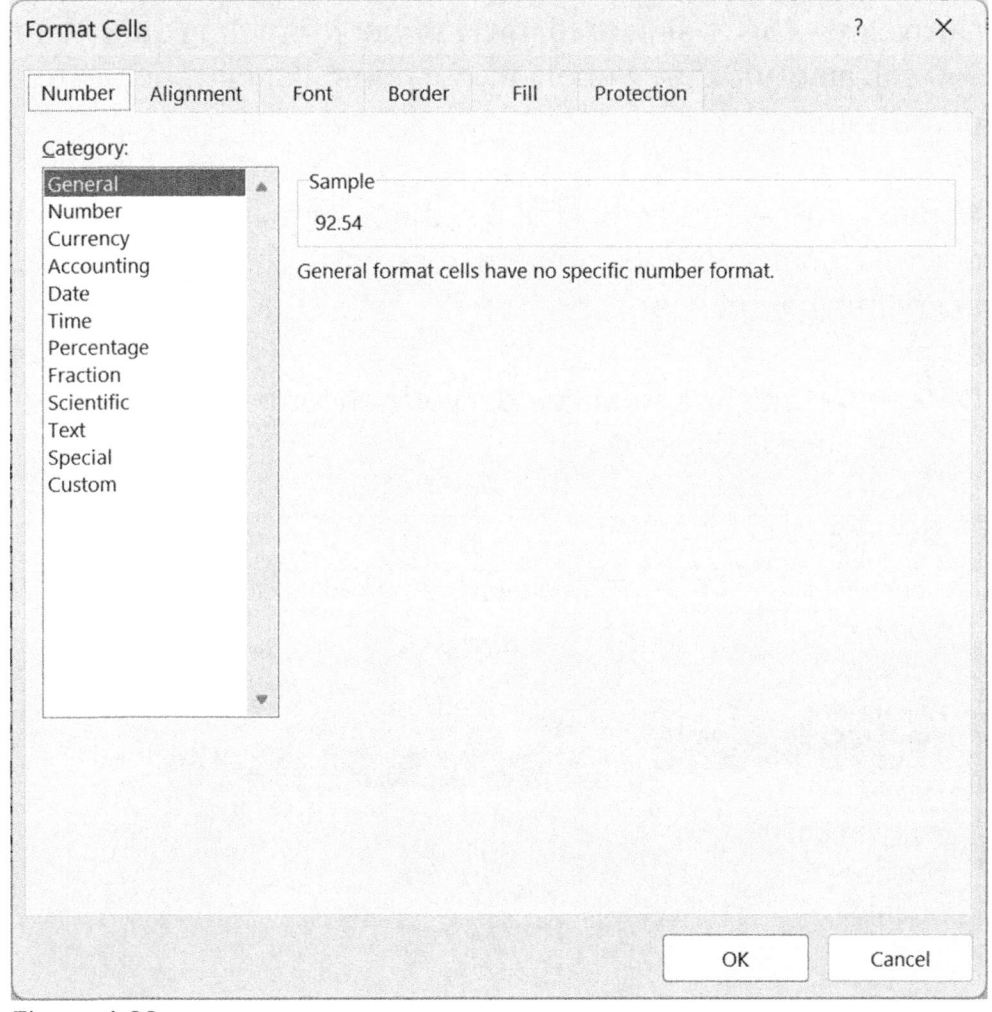

Figure 4.28

As you can see, there are many types of formatting options to choose from and here is what each one of them does.

Chapter 4 – Formatting Your Workbook

- **General** – This setting does not apply any specific formatting to your cells.

- **Number** – Here you can tell Excel how many decimal places to use and also have it format negative numbers in red or in parenthesis.

- **Currency** – This is similar to the Number formatting option, but you can also add the symbol for your particular currency in front of the number.

- **Accounting** – This will line up the currency symbols and decimal points in your column making it easier to view for accounting purposes.

- **Date** – If your cells contain dates, you can format them multiple ways as seen in Figure 4.29.

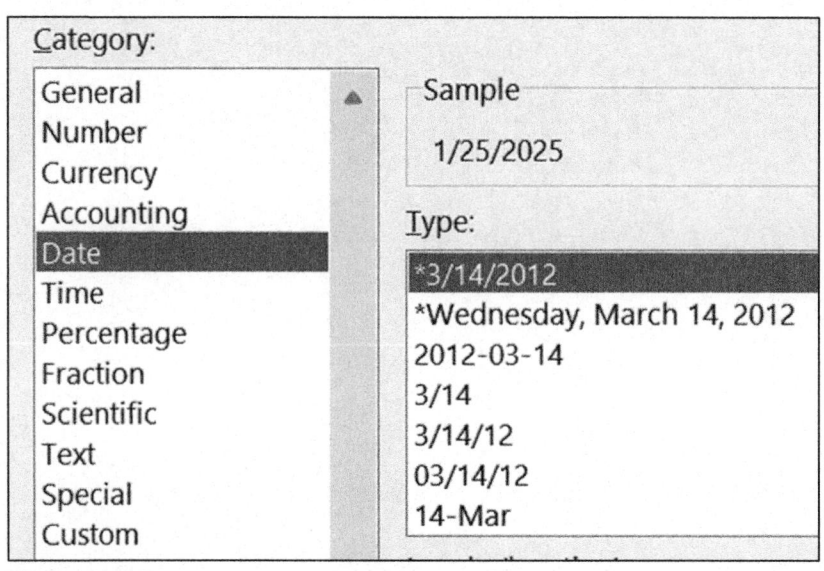

Figure 4.29

- **Time** – This is similar to the Date format setting but applies to cells with time values in them.

112

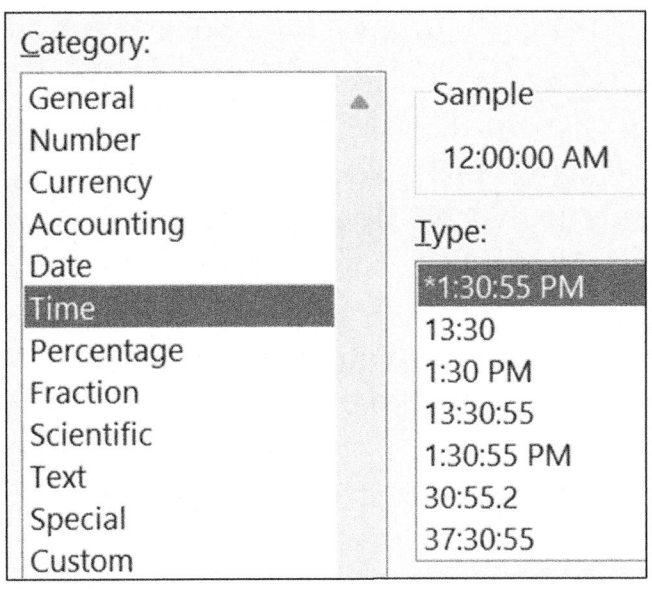

Chapter 4 – Formatting Your Workbook

```
Category:
  General
  Number
  Currency           Sample
  Accounting           12:00:00 AM
  Date
  Time               Type:
  Percentage           *1:30:55 PM
  Fraction             13:30
  Scientific           1:30 PM
  Text                 13:30:55
  Special              1:30:55 PM
  Custom               30:55.2
                       37:30:55
```
Figure 4.30

- **Percentage** – When using percentages in your cells, you can specify how many numbers are used after the decimal point.

- **Fraction** – When using fractions in your cells, you have many choices as to how they are displayed.

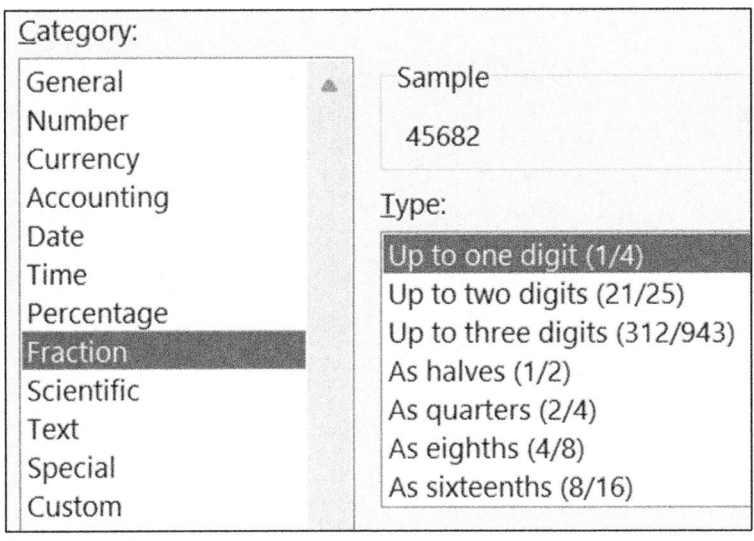

```
Category:
  General
  Number             Sample
  Currency             45682
  Accounting
  Date               Type:
  Time                 Up to one digit (1/4)
  Percentage           Up to two digits (21/25)
  Fraction             Up to three digits (312/943)
  Scientific           As halves (1/2)
  Text                 As quarters (2/4)
  Special              As eighths (4/8)
  Custom               As sixteenths (8/16)
```
Figure 4.31

113

Chapter 4 – Formatting Your Workbook

- **Scientific** – Here you can choose how many decimal places are shown for your numbers.

- **Text** – If you use the Text format for cells with numbers, they will be treated as text only so they will appear exactly how you type them.

- **Special** – This is used for things such as zip codes, phone numbers and social security numbers.

- **Custom** – This option has a variety of formatting choices as you can see in Figure 4.32.

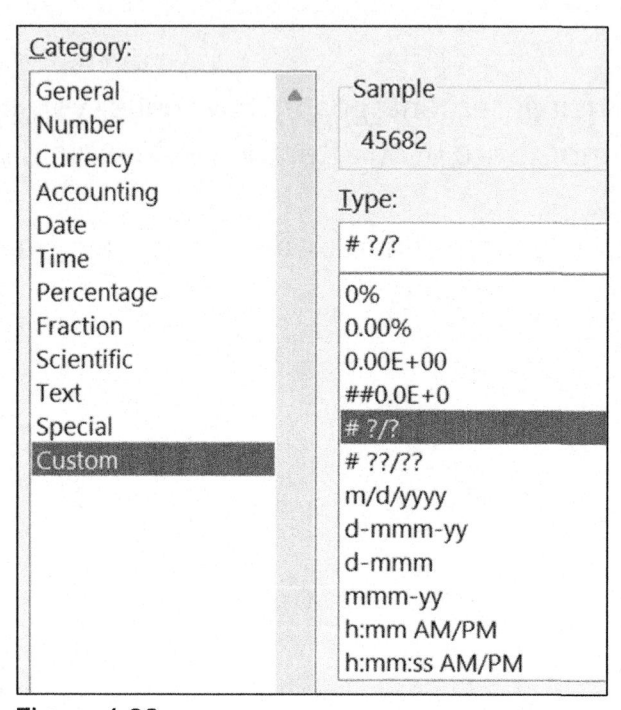

Figure 4.32

Hiding Rows, Columns and Tabs
If you plan on printing your workbook or maybe showing it during a presentation but don't want everything on a worksheet printed or shown to your colleagues, you can easily hide rows, columns and

114

Chapter 4 – Formatting Your Workbook

even tabs and then have them shown again once you are ready to view them.

To hide a row or column, all you need to do is right click on that row or column and choose the *Hide* option. Then you will be able to tell that you have a hidden row or column by the double line between where that row or column used to be shown. You will also notice that the letter is missing as well as seen in figure 4.33 where it goes from column C to column E because column D is hidden.

	A	B	C	E
1	**First Name**	**Last Name**	**Account Number**	**Date Due**
2	Phil	Bailey	2102157	9/3/2024
3	Danny	Burke	8652147	1/2/2024
4	Penelope	Churchill	2623014	4/15/2024
5	Christian	Churchill	2035214	9/17/2025
6	Maria	Cortez	2362411	9/15/2024
7	Mary	Fraser	9201424	4/13/2025
8	Rachel	Ince	8326210	8/7/2025
9	Heather	Kerr	8523624	1/25/2025
10	Kim	Lee	5124715	11/25/2025
11	Jack	McGrath	4236251	6/4/2025
12	Alan	Peake	8236501	10/14/2024
13	Nathan	Pullman	5623147	5/23/2025
14	Joshua	Roberts	5320214	12/2/2025
15	Phil	Thomson	3201201	3/14/2024
16	Theresa	Tucker	1230254	3/15/2024
17	Audrey	Wallace	6920147	2/22/2024

Figure 4.33

Chapter 4 – Formatting Your Workbook

Now when you print or share your workbook, the row or column will be hidden. Just keep in mind that others can unhide your row or column if they notice that it's hidden.

To unhide your row or column, you can simply select the rows or columns on each side of the hidden row or column, right click and choose *Unhide*.

Hiding a worksheet is just as easy as hiding a row or column. To do so, right click the sheet you want to hide and then click on the *Hide* option.

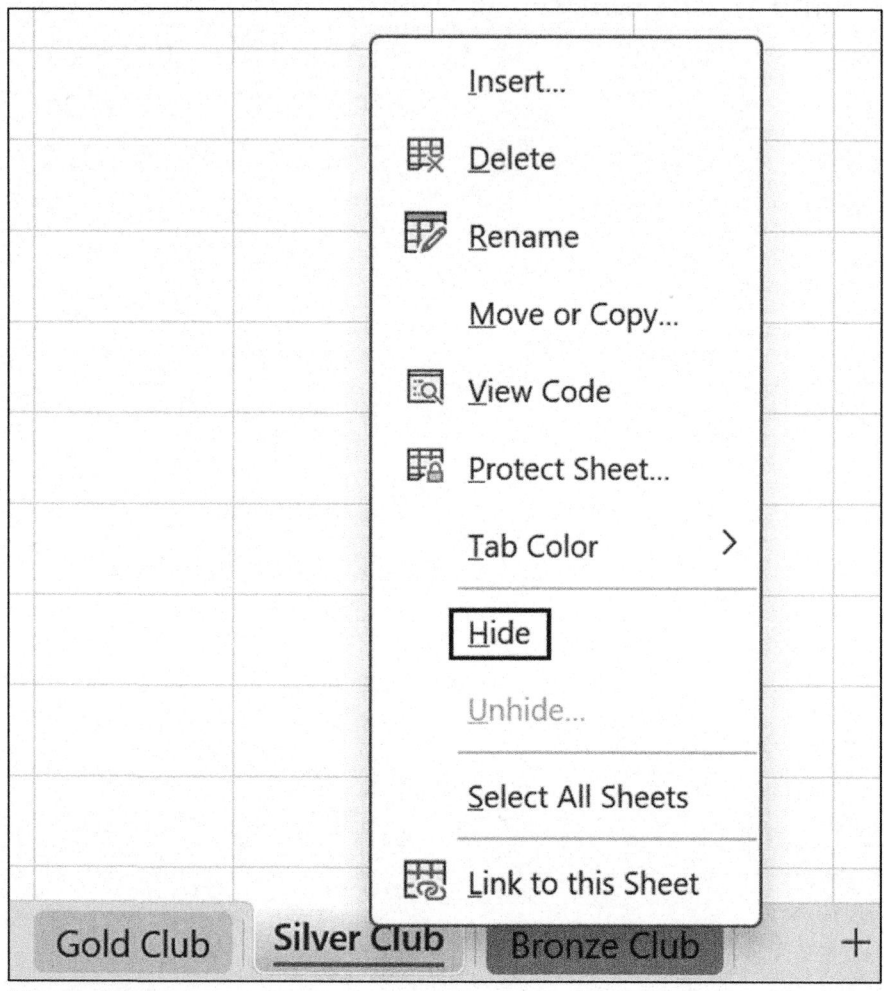

Figure 4.34

Chapter 4 – Formatting Your Workbook

Then to have your worksheet shown with the others, simply right click any other worksheet tab and choose *Unhide.* You will then be prompted to choose which hidden worksheet you want to unhide. If you have more than one hidden you can choose whichever one you like from the list.

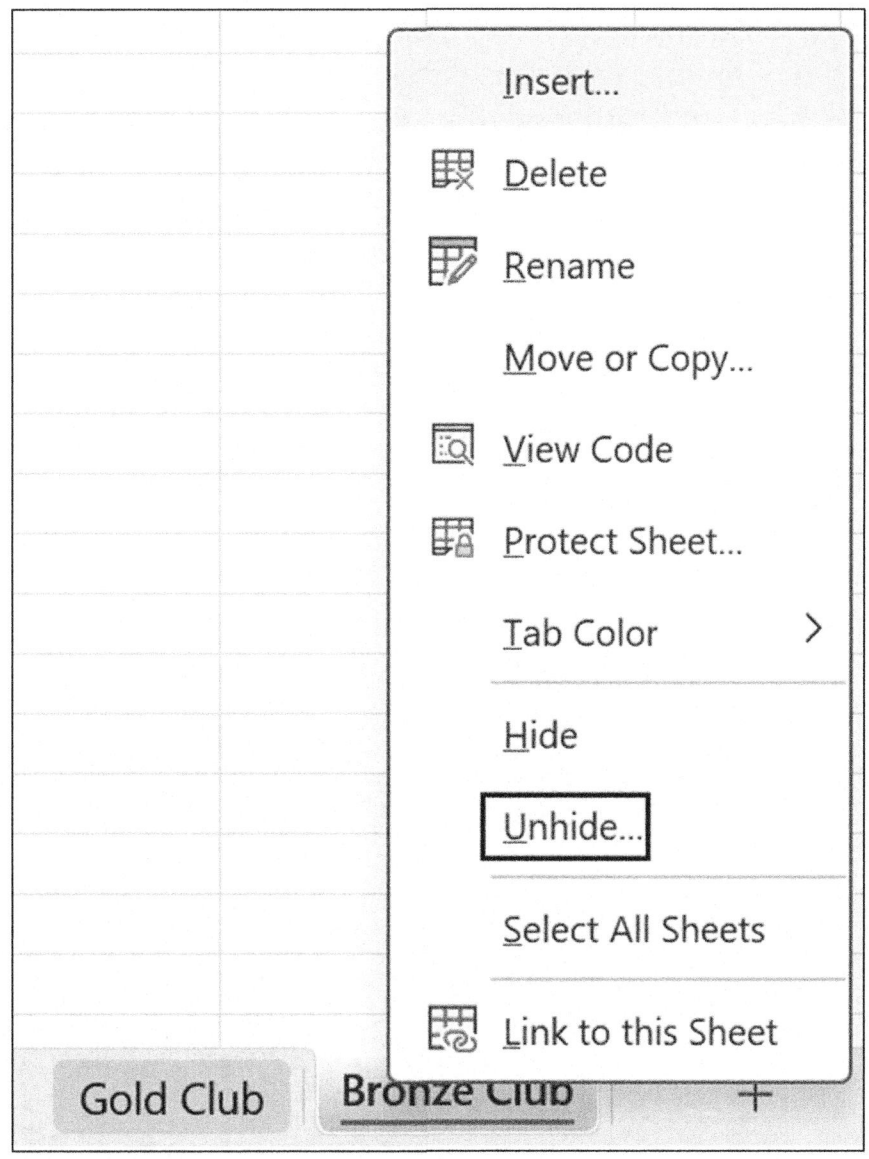

Figure 4.35

Chapter 4 – Formatting Your Workbook

You will need to have at least one worksheet showing in your workbook so you will not be able to hide all the sheets if you try and do so.

Using the Freeze Panes feature
The Freeze Panes feature of Microsoft Excel comes in handy when you have a lot of data and need to keep part of it on the screen while scrolling through the rest of it. This is especially useful when you have column headers and want them to stay at the top of the screen and not disappear when you scroll further down the page. Figure 4.36 shows a worksheet with many rows and if I were to scroll past row 24, then my headers would scroll off the page as well as shown in Figure 4.37.

	A	B	C	D	E	F
1	First Name	Last Name	Account Number	Amount	Date Due	Package Letter
2	Phil	Bailey	2102157	79.34	9/3/2024	A
3	Danny	Burke	8652147	-35.22	1/2/2024	A
4	Penelope	Churchill	2623014	201.51	4/15/2024	B
5	Christian	Churchill	2035214	115.32	9/17/2025	C
6	Maria	Cortez	2362411	-25	9/15/2024	C
7	Mary	Fraser	9201424	89.65	4/13/2025	B
8	Rachel	Ince	8326210	113.24	8/7/2025	A
9	Heather	Kerr	8523624	92.54	1/25/2025	C
10	Kim	Lee	5124715	226.25	11/25/2025	C
11	Jack	McGrath	4236251	88.61	6/4/2025	B
12	Alan	Peake	8236501	98.65	10/14/2024	A
13	Nathan	Pullman	5623147	115.25	5/23/2025	C
14	Joshua	Roberts	5320214	145.21	12/2/2025	B
15	Phil	Thomson	3201201	75.23	3/14/2024	B
16	Theresa	Tucker	1230254	121.14	3/15/2024	A
17	Audrey	Wallace	6920147	68.74	2/22/2024	C
18	Vanessa	Watson	5232148	$121.52	1/23/2025	B
19	Dylan	Bond	4251575	$83.25	7/5/2024	A
20	Nathan	Morgan	6562541	$53.87	8/17/2024	C
21	Christian	Clarkson	4523217	$75.25	5/15/2024	C
22	Victoria	Dyer	4515482	$101.00	9/22/2025	C
23	Phil	Randall	3625145	$112.25	10/15/2024	B
24	Claire	Ogden	3265147	$86.21	12/3/2024	B

Figure 4.36

Chapter 4 – Formatting Your Workbook

	A	B	C	D	E	F
7	Mary	Fraser	9201424	89.65	4/13/2025	B
8	Rachel	Ince	8326210	113.24	8/7/2025	A
9	Heather	Kerr	8523624	92.54	1/25/2025	C
10	Kim	Lee	5124715	226.25	11/25/2025	C
11	Jack	McGrath	4236251	88.61	6/4/2025	B
12	Alan	Peake	8236501	98.65	10/14/2024	A
13	Nathan	Pullman	5623147	115.25	5/23/2025	C
14	Joshua	Roberts	5320214	145.21	12/2/2025	B
15	Phil	Thomson	3201201	75.23	3/14/2024	B
16	Theresa	Tucker	1230254	121.14	3/15/2024	A
17	Audrey	Wallace	6920147	68.74	2/22/2024	C
18	Vanessa	Watson	5232148	$121.52	1/23/2025	B
19	Dylan	Bond	4251575	$83.25	7/5/2024	A
20	Nathan	Morgan	6562541	$53.87	8/17/2024	C
21	Christian	Clarkson	4523217	$75.25	5/15/2024	C
22	Victoria	Dyer	4515482	$101.00	9/22/2025	C
23	Phil	Randall	3625145	$112.25	10/15/2024	B
24	Claire	Ogden	3265147	$86.21	12/3/2024	B
25	Jan	Clark	9562147	$97.24	8/27/2025	C
26	Connor	Mathis	3265147	$118.32	8/6/2025	C
27	Jessica	McGrath	2233517	$198.98	9/17/2025	B

Figure 4.37

But if I enable the *Freeze Top Row* option as seen in Figure 4.38, the top row with my headers will always stay at the top no matter how far down I scroll as seen in Figure 4.39.

Chapter 4 – Formatting Your Workbook

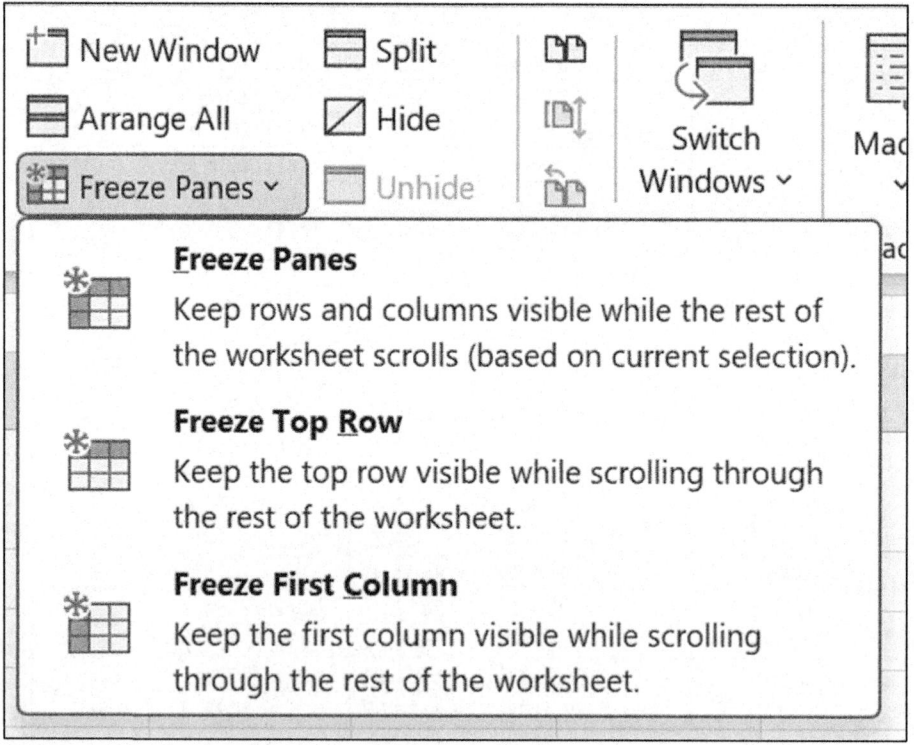

Figure 4.38

	A	B	C	D	E	F
1	First Name	Last Name	Account Number	Amount	Date Due	Package Letter
17	Audrey	Wallace	6920147	68.74	2/22/2024	C
18	Vanessa	Watson	5232148	$121.52	1/23/2025	B
19	Dylan	Bond	4251575	$83.25	7/5/2024	A
20	Nathan	Morgan	6562541	$53.87	8/17/2024	C
21	Christian	Clarkson	4523217	$75.25	5/15/2024	C
22	Victoria	Dyer	4515482	$101.00	9/22/2025	C
23	Phil	Randall	3625145	$112.25	10/15/2024	B
24	Claire	Ogden	3265147	$86.21	12/3/2024	B
25	Jan	Clark	9562147	$97.24	8/27/2025	C
26	Connor	Mathis	3265147	$118.32	8/6/2025	C
27	Jessica	McGrath	2233517	$198.98	9/17/2025	B
28	Brian	Randall	9532214	$58.21	11/5/2024	B
29	Natalie	Baker	9215714	$136.84	1/26/2024	B
30	Cameron	Welch	3215412	$147.98	11/15/2024	C
31	Anthony	Lewis	8762514	$26.25	5/4/2025	A
32	Luke	Simpson	5621514	$89.27	3/2/2024	A
33	Amy	Avery	7563214	$139.75	2/19/2025	C

Figure 4.39

Chapter 4 – Formatting Your Workbook

Merging Cells

As I have mentioned before, when you type data into a cell, it will spill over into the next cell if the information is too long for the width of the cell. If you stretch out the width of that cell to make it fit, you will also be stretching out the other cells in that column which might not be what you want to do.

I have added a title to my worksheet in row 1 and as you can see, it appears to take up columns A through D even though it's really only in column A.

	A	B	C	D	E	F
1	**Snobby Golf Club Member Dues**					
2	First Name	Last Name	Account Number	Amount	Date Due	Package Letter
3	Phil	Bailey	2102157	79.34	9/3/2024	A
4	Danny	Burke	8652147	-35.22	1/2/2024	A
5	Penelope	Churchill	2623014	201.51	4/15/2024	B

Figure 4.40

I can use the *Merge & Center* option from the *Home* tab to make cell A1 take up the space all the way to cell F1 without affecting the other rows or columns.

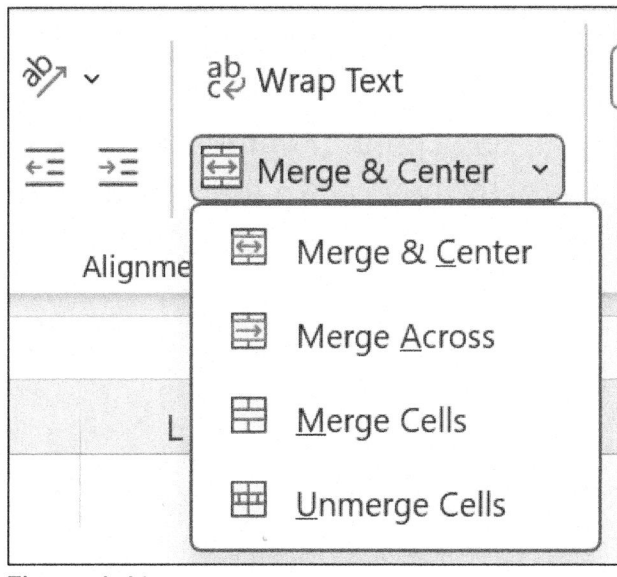

Figure 4.41

Chapter 4 – Formatting Your Workbook

To do so, I just need to highlight the range of cells that I want my data to be merged into as seen in Figure 4.42.

	A	B	C	D	E	F	G
1	**Snobby Golf Club Member Dues**						
2	First Name	Last Name	Account Number	Amount	Date Due	Package Letter	
3	Phil	Bailey	2102157	79.34	9/3/2024	A	
4	Danny	Burke	8652147	-35.22	1/2/2024	A	
5	Penelope	Churchill	2623014	201.51	4/15/2024	B	
6	Christian	Churchill	2035214	115.32	9/17/2025	C	
7	Maria	Cortez	2362411	-25	9/15/2024	C	

Figure 4.42

Now when I choose the Merge & Center option, cell A1 is now merged all the way over to cell F1 and it appears to be one single cell. This also means that I cannot add any data to cells B1 through F1 since they have all been merged with cell A1.

	A	B	C	D	E	F
1	**Snobby Golf Club Member Dues**					
2	First Name	Last Name	Account Number	Amount	Date Due	Package Letter
3	Phil	Bailey	2102157	79.34	9/3/2024	A
4	Danny	Burke	8652147	-35.22	1/2/2024	A
5	Penelope	Churchill	2623014	201.51	4/15/2024	B
6	Christian	Churchill	2035214	115.32	9/17/2025	C
7	Maria	Cortez	2362411	-25	9/15/2024	C

Figure 4.43

You can also use the *Merge Across* option to do the same thing without centering the contents of the main cell if that is your goal.

Chapter 5 – Page Layout and Printing

If you only plan on using Excel on your computer and don't plan on ever printing your workbooks or converting them to PDF files for example, then page setup is not as critical as if you were to be doing these things.

When you have complex worksheets with lots of data, you will find that it can be hard to fit your rows and columns on a page, so things look correct when printing or exporting your spreadsheet. Knowing how to use the page layout features is critical if you plan on printing or sharing your workbooks.

Page Setup
The Page Setup group under the *Page Layout* tab has most of the tools you will need to get your spreadsheet ready for printing or exporting.

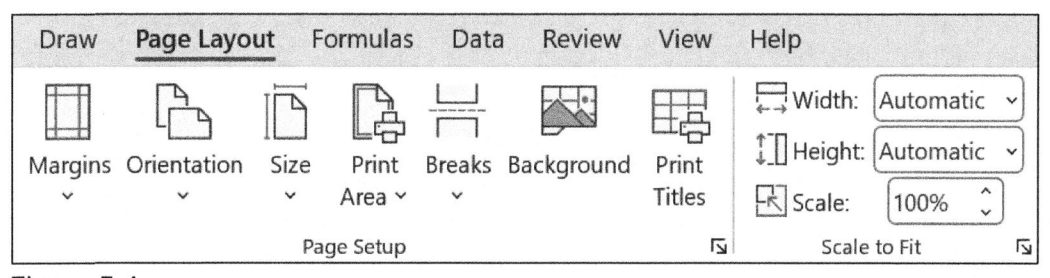

Figure 5.1

If you click on the arrow at the lower right corner of the group, you will see some additional options.

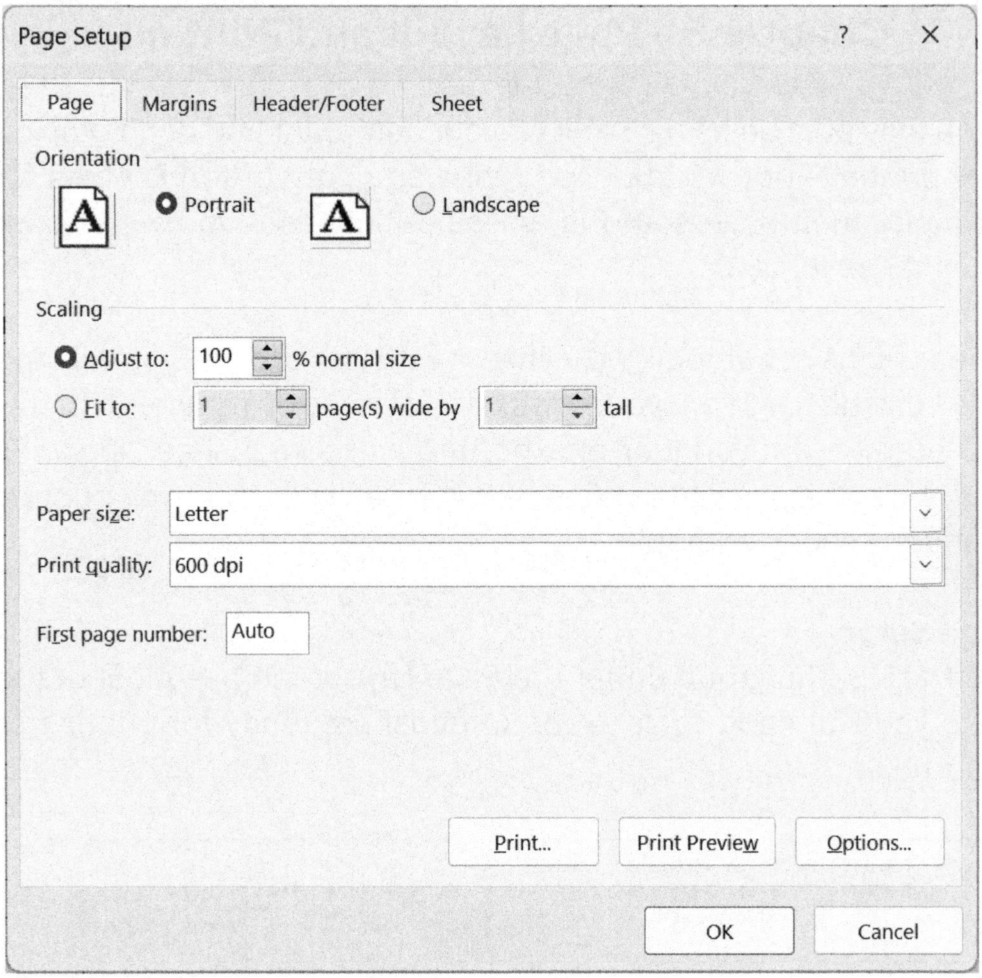

Chapter 5 – Page Layout and Printing

Figure 5.2

Many people like to use landscape orientation when printing spreadsheets because you can fit more columns on the page. It's easier to read printed spreadsheets when you can see all the columns on one page compared to having all your rows on one page.

Setting margins is another way to help you fit all your data on a page. Just be sure not to go too small so it gets cut off or doesn't look right when printing.

Be careful when using the *Adjust to* and *Fit to* options because if you make a large spreadsheet fit on one page, it will end up being

Chapter 5 – Page Layout and Printing

so small that you cannot read anything on it. You can play around with the number of pages having it set to fit to until it looks the way you want it to. You can click the *Print Preview* button to see how it will look when it's printed out.

The *Size* button that you can see in Figure 5.1 will let you choose your paper size and then adjust the print preview to match so you can see how your spreadsheet will really look when printed on the actual size paper you plan to use.

Page Breaks
When printing your workbook, it's nice to be able to see how your pages will be split up on the printed sheets so you have an idea of how the print job will look before actually printing your spreadsheet.

Sure, you can use the print preview feature but if you want to get an overview of what data is on what page, you can switch to the *Page Break Preview* from the *View* tab.

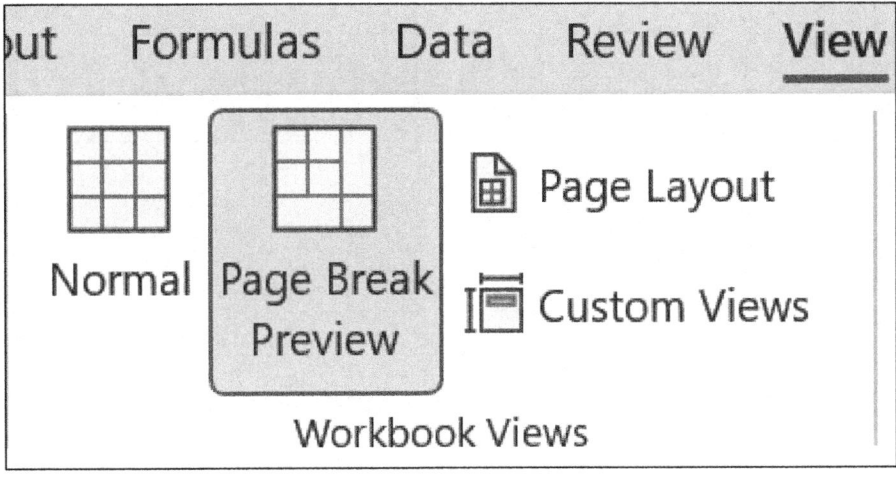

Figure 5.3

When you switch to the Page Break Preview view, you will see all your pages in one place with dotted blue lines separating the

Chapter 5 – Page Layout and Printing

actual pages. They will also be labeled as Page 1, Page 2 and so on. This also tells you the order in which your pages will be printed. Figure 5.4 shows that to print this worksheet, it will take 4 sheets of paper in its current configuration.

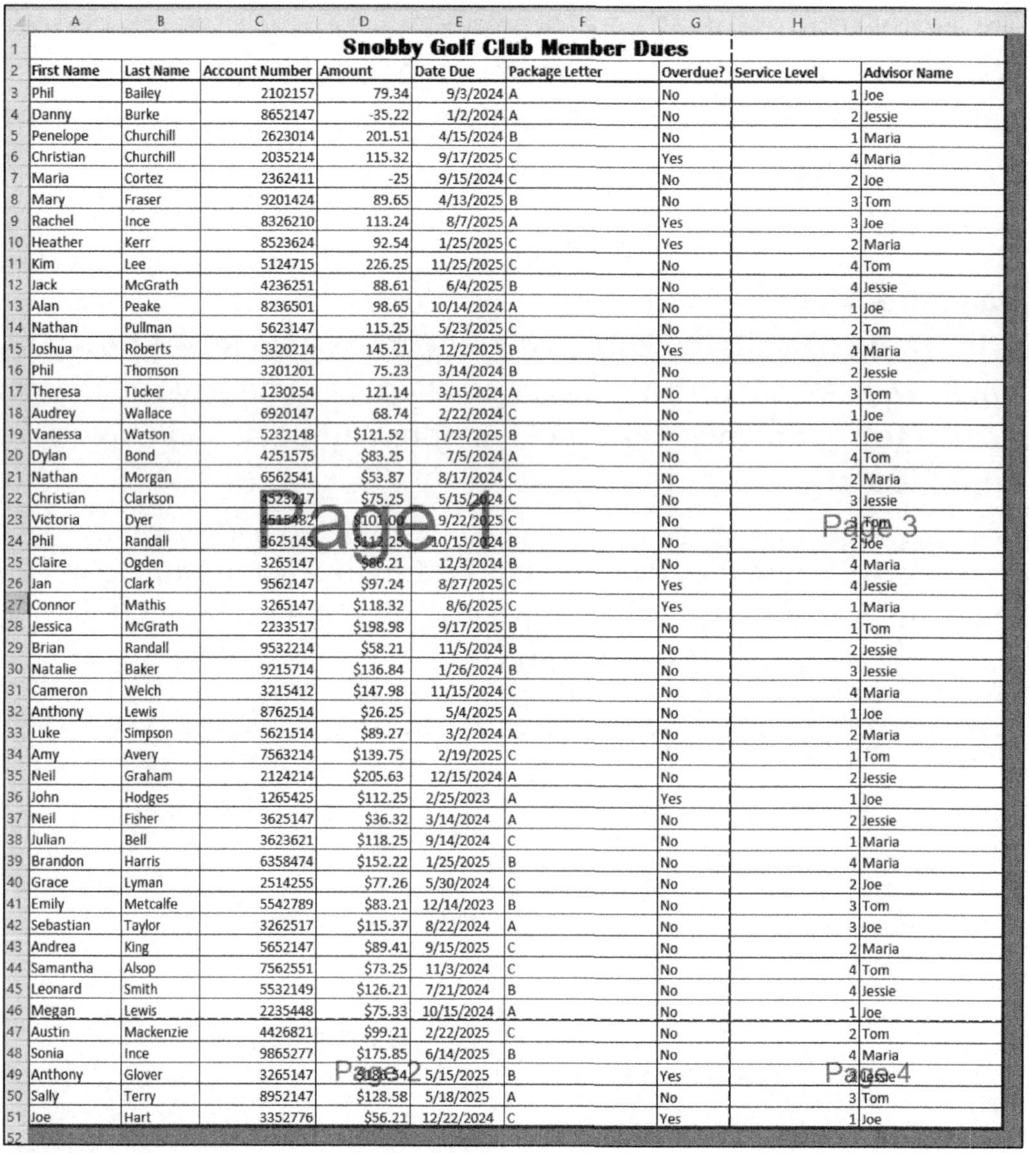

Figure 5.4

You can however switch the order of your pages by going back to the Page Setup options as seen in Figure 5.2 and going to the *Page order* section on the *Sheet* tab.

126

Chapter 5 – Page Layout and Printing

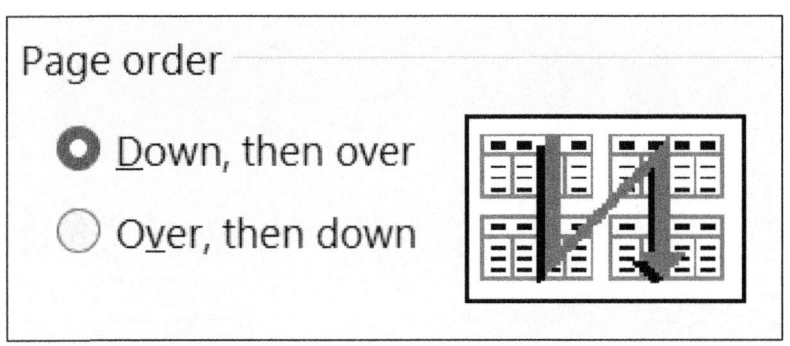

Figure 5.5

While in the page preview mode, you can adjust your row and column sizes to make them fit on specific pages if you can do so without having to shrink them down too much to where you can't see all your data.

You can also adjust your margins etc. and then come back here and see if the change was enough to get the data you want on the page you want it to be on.

Printing Worksheets and Workbooks
If you plan on printing your spreadsheets, then you should know that there are several ways to go about it and you can really customize how your print jobs will look on paper.

To start the printing process, you can click on the *File* tab and then on *Print*. Figure 5.6 shows all the available printing options that you have so you can make sure your print job comes out correctly.

Chapter 5 – Page Layout and Printing

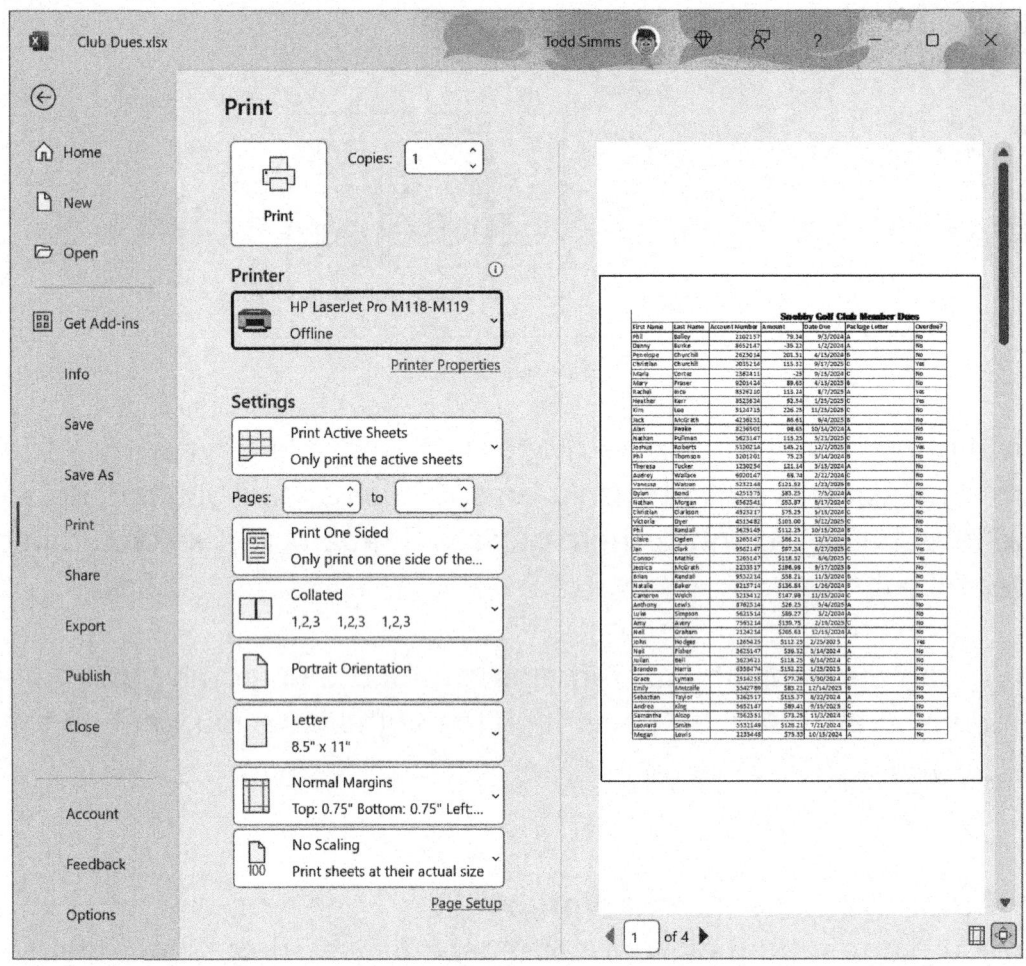

Figure 5.6

At the top of the window, you have the *Copies* selection box where you can specify how many copies of each page you want to have printed. Then there is the *Printer* drop down box where you can choose which printer you want to send the print job to if you have more than one.

Clicking on the *Printer Properties* link will open the settings for your specific printer where you can do things such as change paper trays, set up double sided printing and set print quality options. The settings you see here will vary depending on your printer's make and model.

Chapter 5 – Page Layout and Printing

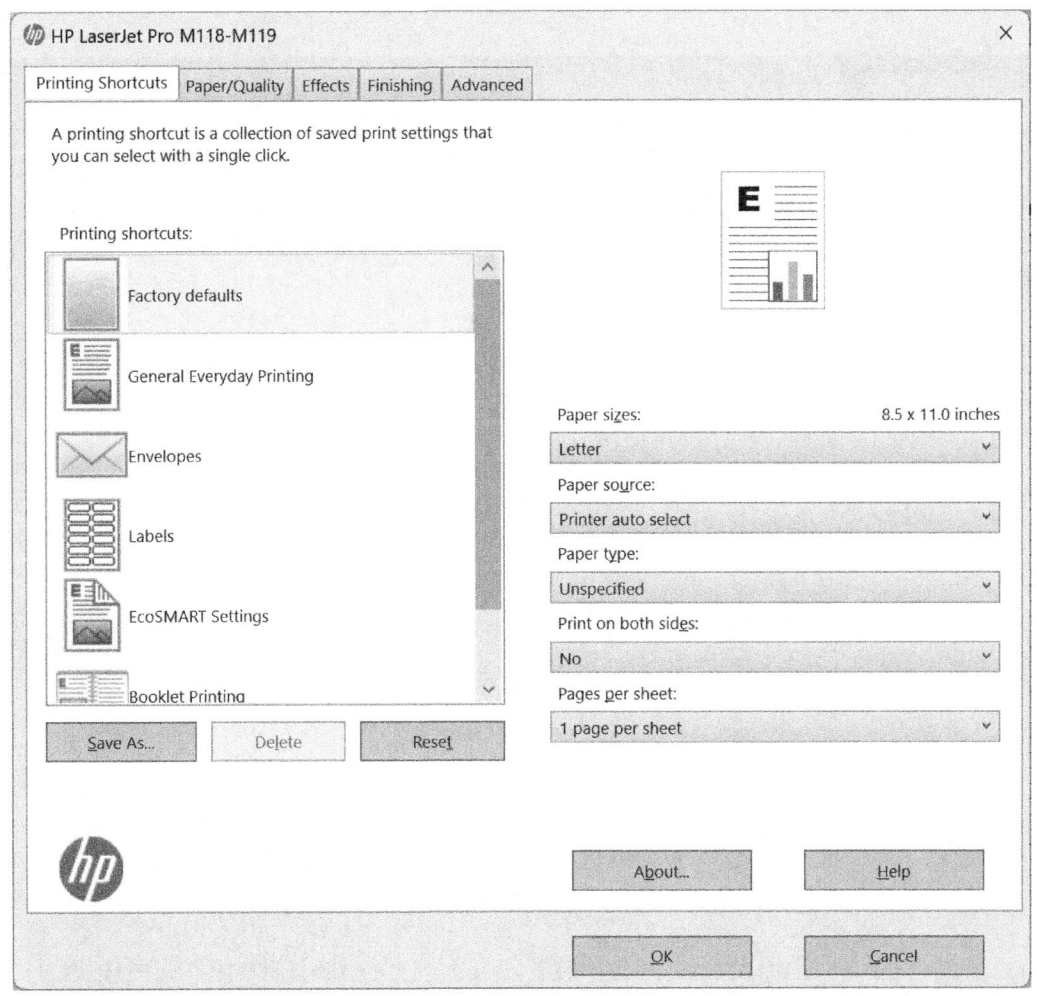

Figure 5.7

Under the Printer Settings dropdown, you can then choose which part of your spreadsheet you want to print as shown in Figure 5.8.

Chapter 5 – Page Layout and Printing

Settings

Print Active Sheets
Only print the active sheets

Print Active Sheets
Only print the active sheets

Print Entire Workbook
Print the entire workbook

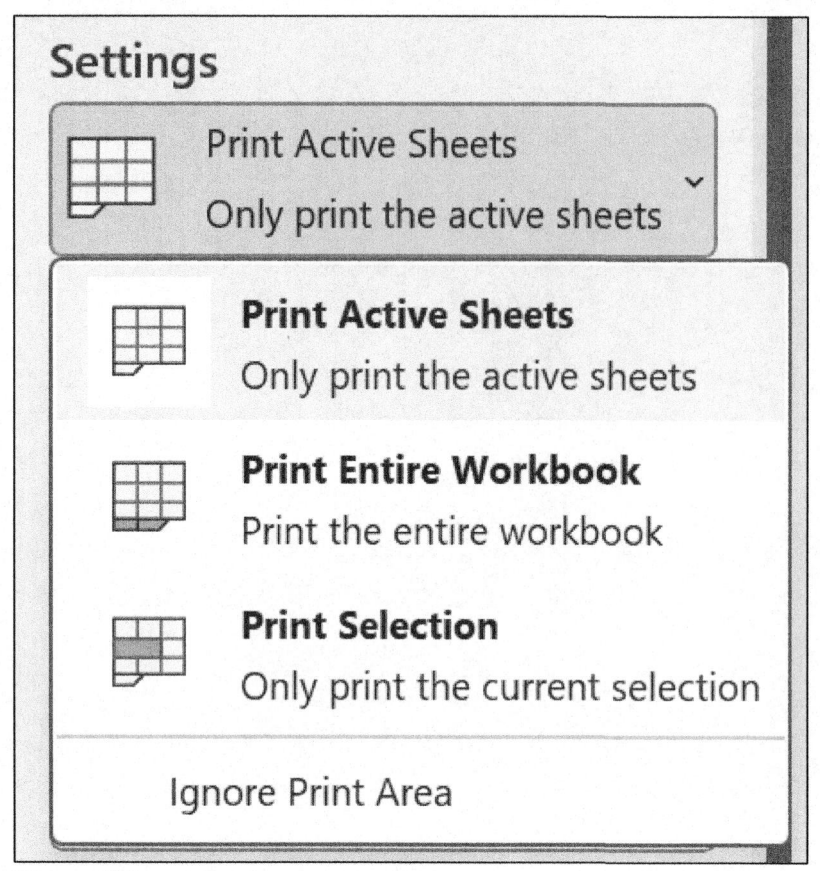

Print Selection
Only print the current selection

Ignore Print Area

Figure 5.8

You can print just the worksheet you were on when you went to the print settings, print all the worksheets within your workbook, or print just a range of cells that you select beforehand.

If you print the entire workbook, be sure to check out the print preview to make sure that everything looks correct because your print job can get complicated if you have multiple worksheets with a lot of data.

The *Print Selection* option comes in very handy when you just need to print a specific selection of data. Figure 5.9 shows that I have highlighted cells A1 through E10 because this is the section of my worksheet that I want to print because I do not need the rest of the data printed at this time.

Chapter 5 – Page Layout and Printing

	A	B	C	D	E	F	G	H	I
1				Snobby Golf Club Member Dues					
2	First Name	Last Name	Account Number	Amount	Date Due	Package Letter	Overdue?	Service Level	Advisor Name
3	Phil	Bailey	2102157	79.34	9/3/2024	A	No	1	Joe
4	Danny	Burke	8652147	-35.22	1/2/2024	A	No	2	Jessie
5	Penelope	Churchill	2623014	201.51	4/15/2024	B	No	1	Maria
6	Christian	Churchill	2035214	115.32	9/17/2025	C	Yes	4	Maria
7	Maria	Cortez	2362411	-25	9/15/2024	C	No	2	Joe
8	Mary	Fraser	9201424	89.65	4/13/2025	B	No	3	Tom
9	Rachel	Ince	8326210	113.24	8/7/2025	A	Yes	3	Joe
10	Heather	Kerr	8523624	92.54	1/25/2025	C	Yes	2	Maria
11	Kim	Lee	5124715	226.25	11/25/2025	C	No	4	Tom
12	Jack	McGrath	4236251	88.61	6/4/2025	B	No	4	Jessie

Figure 5.9

When I go to the printing options and choose Print Selection, you can see in the print preview that only the cells I have selected appear. This means that my selected range is the only part of my worksheet that will be printed.

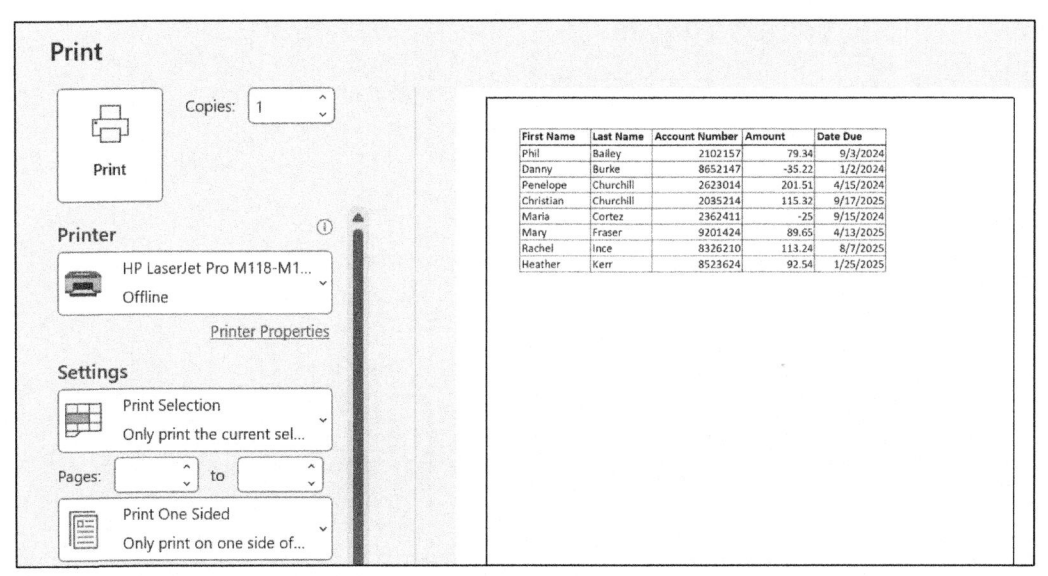

Figure 5.10

Going back to the print settings, you can also choose which pages you want to be printed by typing in the first and last page numbers in the *Pages* section.

Chapter 5 – Page Layout and Printing

Settings

- Print Selection — Only print the current sel...
- Pages: 2 to 5
- Print One Sided — Only print on one side of...
- Collated — 1,2,3 1,2,3 1,2,3
- Portrait Orientation
- Letter — 8.5" x 11"
- Normal Margins — Top: 0.75" Bottom: 0.75" L...
- No Scaling — Print sheets at their actual...

Page Setup

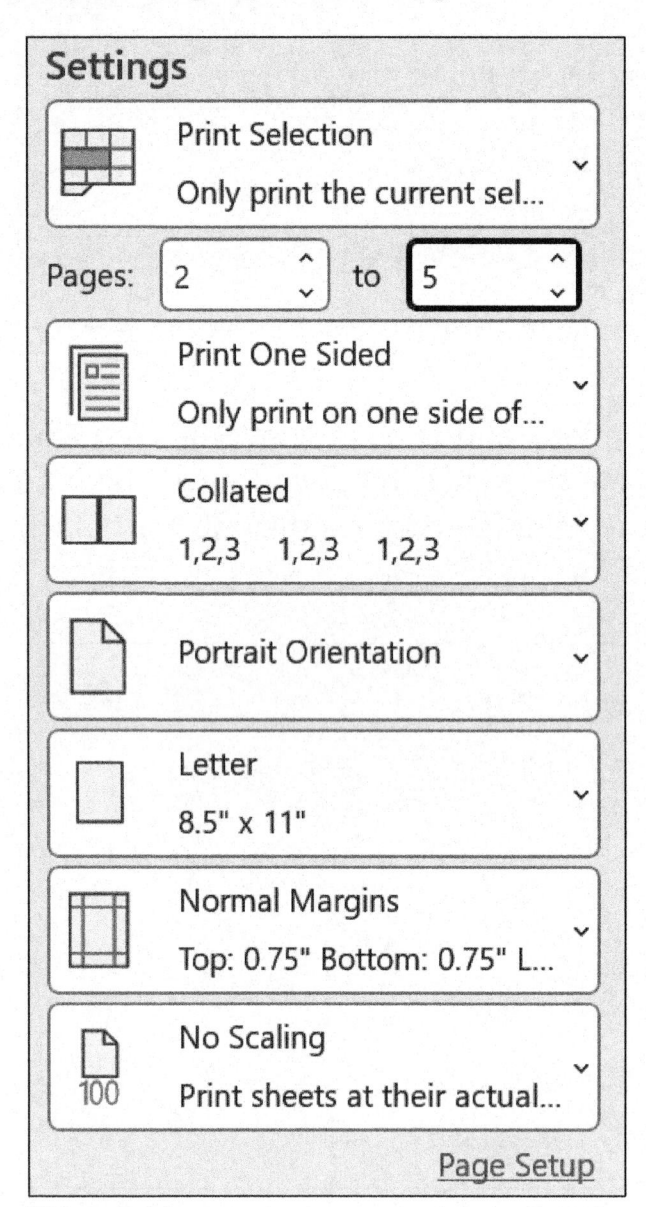

Figure 5.11

There are other handy settings here as well such as the ability to change the page orientation from portrait to landscape, change the paper size, and change the page margins.

The *scaling* option can be used to help you fit your data on the page, so things look correct when printing your spreadsheet. As you can see in Figure 5.12, there are several options you can use to help make things fit.

Chapter 5 – Page Layout and Printing

Settings

Print Selection
Only print the current sel...

Pages: 2 to 5

Print One Sided
Only print on one side of...

Collated
1,2,3   1,2,3   1,2,3

Portrait Orientation

Letter
8.5" x 11"

Normal Margins
Top: 0.75" Bottom: 0.75" L...

No Scaling
Print sheets at their actual...

Page Setup

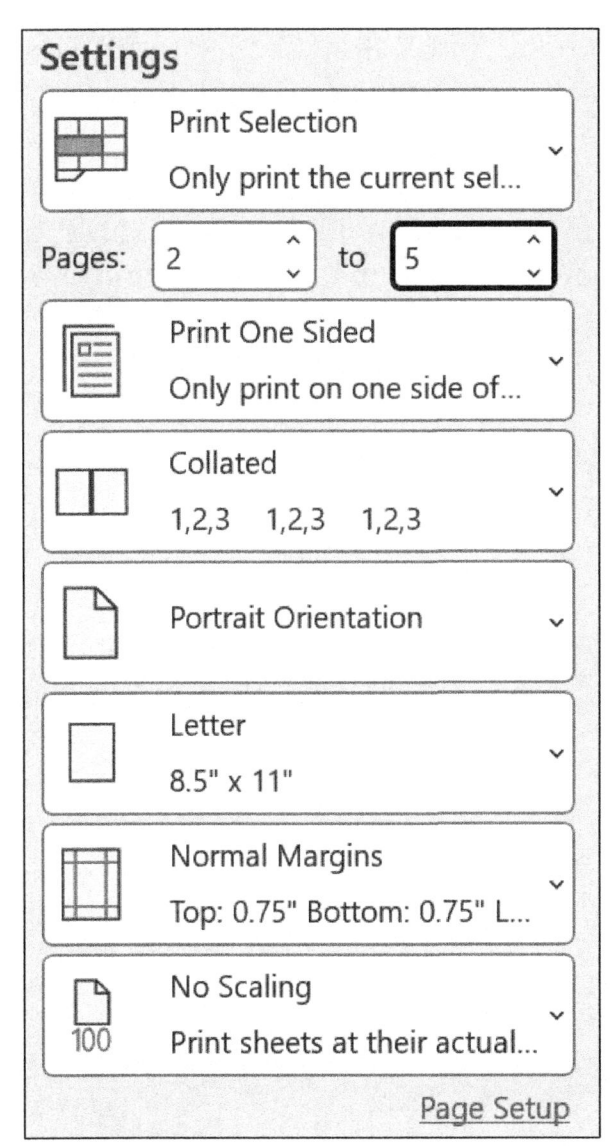

Figure 5.12

Finally, you can click on the *Page Setup* link at the bottom of the settings to be taken back to the page setup options that you have already seen.

Creating PDF Files

One common way to share your workbook rather than printing it out or sharing it as an Excel file is to create a PDF version of it. This way you can send your spreadsheet to others in a preformatted file

Chapter 5 – Page Layout and Printing

that they will not be able to edit. And if they need to print your spreadsheet, it will already be configured with the right data on the right pages.

There are a couple of ways to create a PDF version of your spreadsheet in Excel. One way is to go to the *File* menu and then click on the *Export* option. Then make sure that *Create PDF/XPS Document* is selected and then click the *Create PDF/XPS* button.

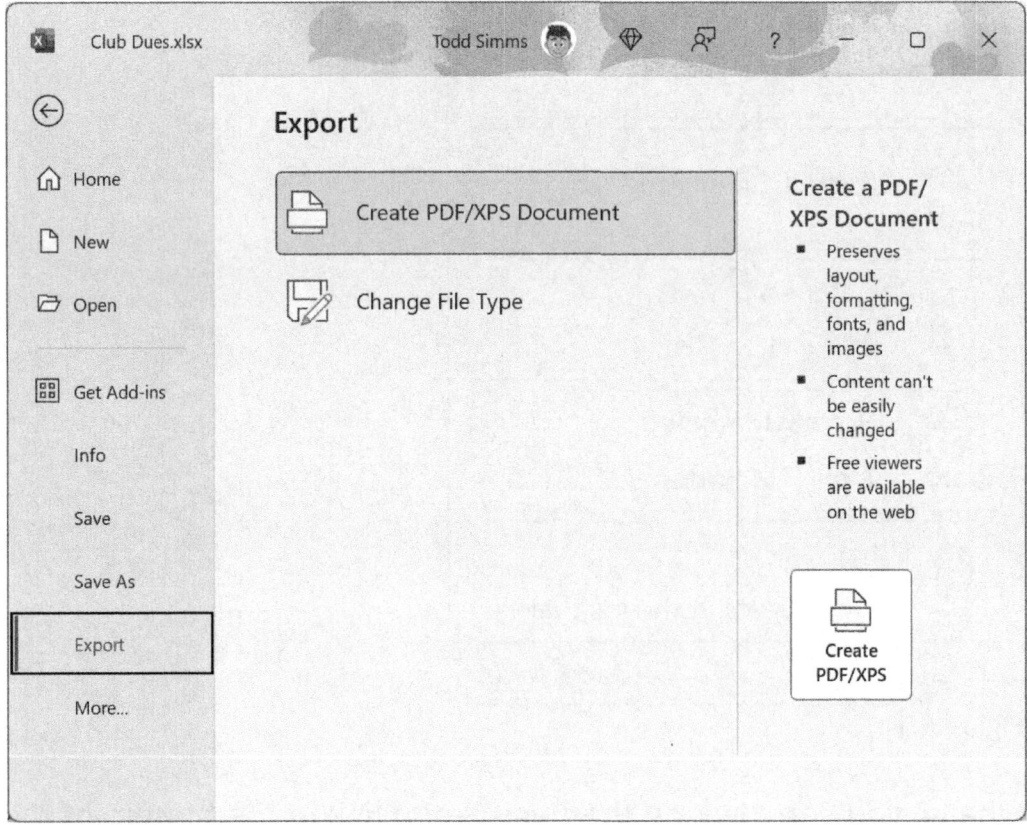

Figure 5.13

You will then be prompted to choose a location and name for your PDF file. By default, Excel will name the PDF file with the same name as your Excel file. You can then choose your quality level by selecting standard or minimum size.

Chapter 5 – Page Layout and Printing

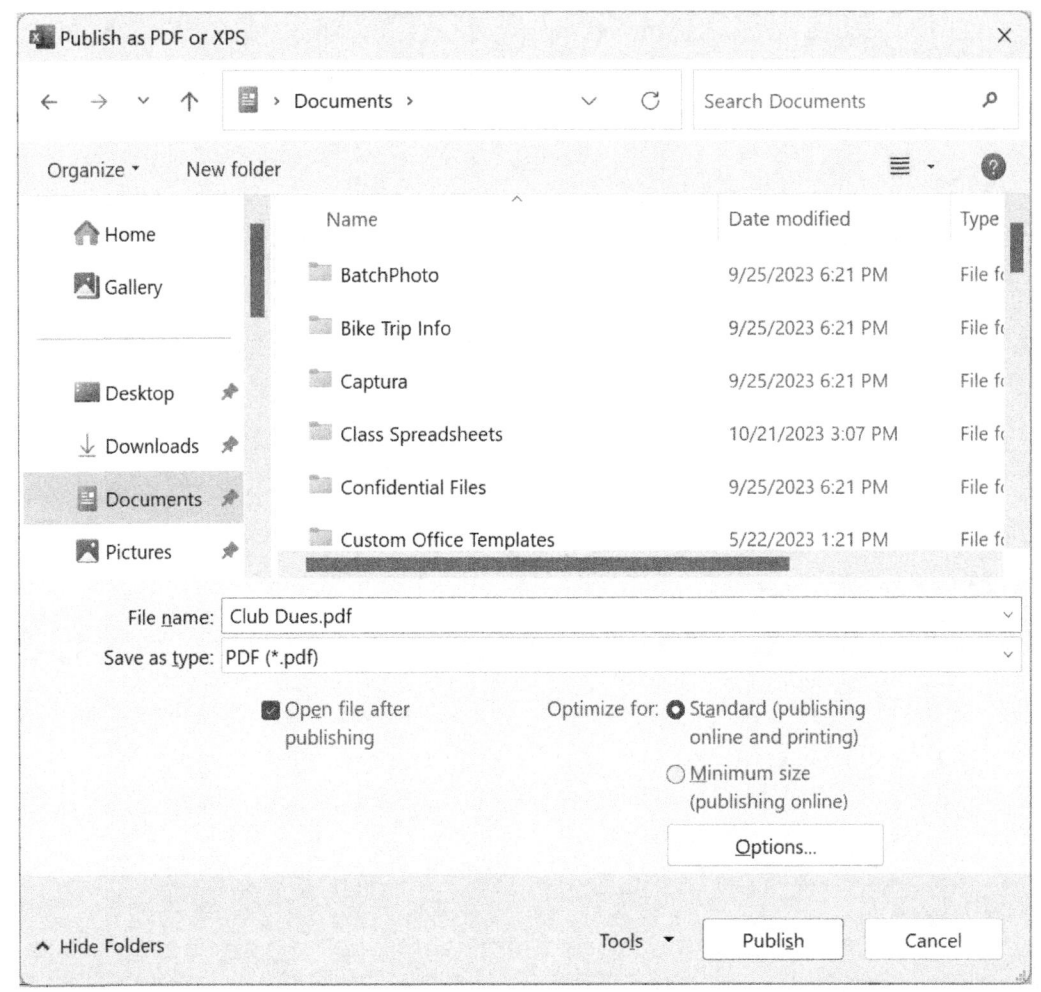

Figure 5.14

If you click on the *Options* button, you can choose what pages you wish to add to your PDF as well as if you want to include the worksheet you are currently on or the entire workbook. You can also have just a selected range of cells added to your PDF like you saw in the section on printing.

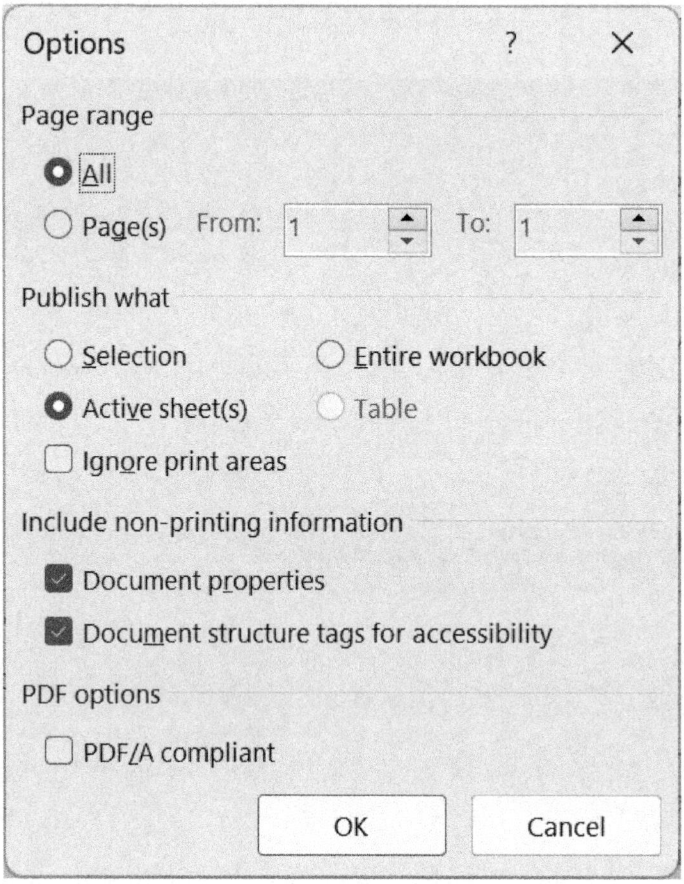

Chapter 5 – Page Layout and Printing

Figure 5.15

One thing you will need to do before using the export option is make sure your data is laid out correctly on the appropriate pages because you will not have the same page setup options that you saw for printing your worksheet.

Figure 5.16 shows that only part of my sheet made it on the first page and that the last two columns were placed on a different page (Figure 5.17).

Chapter 5 – Page Layout and Printing

		Snobby Golf Club Member Dues				
First Name	Last Name	Account Number	Amount	Date Due	Package Letter	Overdue?
Phil	Bailey	2102157	79.34	9/3/2024	A	No
Danny	Burke	8652147	-35.22	1/2/2024	A	No
Penelope	Churchill	2623014	201.51	4/15/2024	B	No
Christian	Churchill	2035214	115.32	9/17/2025	C	Yes
Maria	Cortez	2362411	-25	9/15/2024	C	No
Mary	Fraser	9201424	89.65	4/13/2025	B	No
Rachel	Ince	8326210	113.24	8/7/2025	A	Yes
Heather	Kerr	8523624	92.54	1/25/2025	C	Yes
Kim	Lee	5124715	226.25	11/25/2025	C	No
Jack	McGrath	4236251	88.61	6/4/2025	B	No
Alan	Peake	8236501	98.65	10/14/2024	A	No
Nathan	Pullman	5623147	115.25	5/23/2025	C	No
Joshua	Roberts	5320214	145.21	12/2/2025	B	Yes
Phil	Thomson	3201201	75.23	3/14/2024	B	No
Theresa	Tucker	1230254	121.14	3/15/2024	A	No
Audrey	Wallace	6920147	68.74	2/22/2024	C	No
Vanessa	Watson	5232148	$121.52	1/23/2025	B	No

Figure 5.16

Service Level	Advisor Name
1	Joe
2	Jessie
1	Maria
4	Maria
2	Joe
3	Tom
3	Joe
2	Maria
4	Tom
4	Jessie
1	Joe
2	Tom
4	Maria
2	Jessie

Figure 5.17

Another way to create PDFs from your Excel worksheets is to use the *Microsoft Print to PDF* virtual printer. This comes standard with Windows and can be used with almost any program you have installed on your computer to print to PDF files.

To use the Print to PDF feature, simply go to the print settings just like you would to print your spreadsheet on your physical printer

Chapter 5 – Page Layout and Printing

but choose the Microsoft Print to PDF printer from the dropdown list (Figure 5.18).

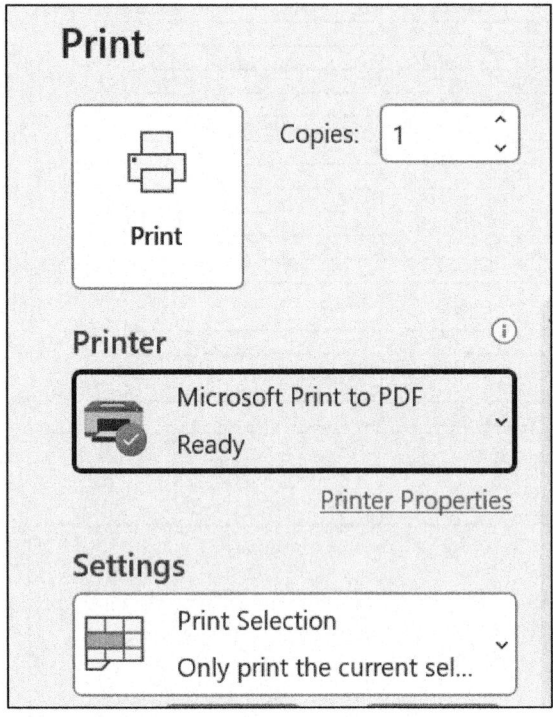

Figure 5.18

Then you can go through all the same print settings as if you were printing your spreadsheet on paper.

After you have everything looking good, click on the *Print* button and you will be prompted to choose a location to save your PDF and you will need to type in a name for the PDF file as well. As you can see in Figure 5.19, you do not have the same quality selections as you do when using the export option but for the most part, you won't notice a difference especially if you do not have images or other graphics within your sheet.

Chapter 5 – Page Layout and Printing

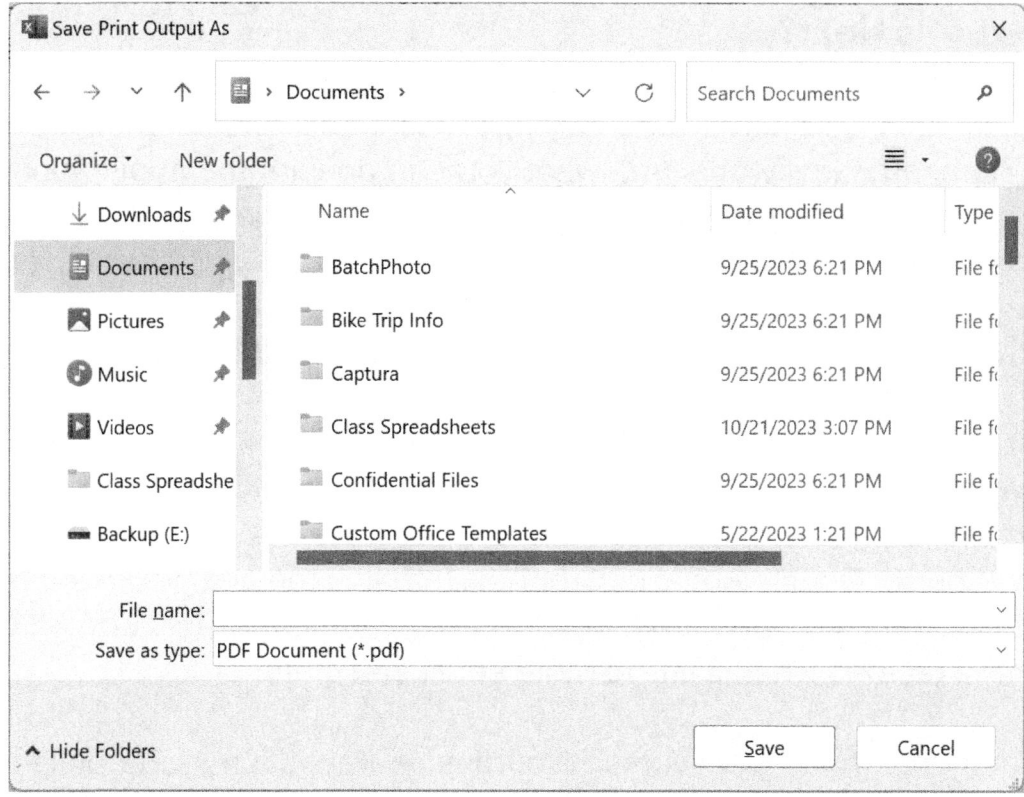

Figure 5.19

What's Next?

Now that you have read through this book and learned how Microsoft Excel works and what you can do with the application, you might be wondering what you should do next. Well, that depends on where you want to go. Are you happy with what you have learned, or do you want to further your knowledge of the available Microsoft Office apps such as Word and PowerPoint?

If you do want to expand your knowledge and computers in general, then you can look for some more advanced books on basic computers or focus on a specific technology such as Windows, Google Apps, or DropBox, if that is the path you choose to follow. Focus on mastering the basics, and then apply what you have learned when going to more advanced material.

There are many great video resources as well, such as Pluralsight or CBT Nuggets, which offer online subscriptions to training videos of every type imaginable. YouTube is also a great source for instructional videos if you know what to search for.

If you are content with being a proficient Excel user who knows more than your coworkers and friends, then just keep on practicing what you have learned. Don't be afraid to poke around with some of the settings and tools that you normally don't use and see if you can figure out what they do without having to research it since learning by doing is the most effective method to gain new skills.

Thanks for reading **Microsoft Excel for Seniors Made Easy**. You can also check out the other books in the Made Easy series for additional computer related information and training. You can get more information on my other books on my Computers Made Easy Book Series website.

https://www.madeeasybookseries.com/

What's Next?

What's Next?

You should also check out my computer tips website, as well as follow it on Facebook to find more information on all kinds of computer topics. I also have online training courses you can take at your own pace.

www.onlinecomputertips.com
https://www.facebook.com/OnlineComputerTips/
http://madeeasytraining.com

About the Author

James Bernstein has been working with various companies in the IT field for over 20 years, managing technologies such as SAN and NAS storage, VMware, backups, Windows Servers, Active Directory, DNS, DHCP, Networking, Microsoft Office, Photoshop, Premiere, Exchange, and more.

He has obtained certifications from Microsoft, VMware, CompTIA, ShoreTel, and SNIA, and continues to strive to learn new technologies to further his knowledge on a variety of subjects.

He is also the founder of the website onlinecomputertips.com, which offers its readers valuable information on topics such as Windows, networking, hardware, software, and troubleshooting. James writes much of the content himself and adds new content on a regular basis. The site was started in 2005 and is still going strong today.

Printed in Great Britain
by Amazon